Prayer Power Unlimited

By
J. Oswald Sanders

MOODY PRESS
CHICAGO

All scripture quotations, except those noted
otherwise, are from the *New American
Standard Bible*, © 1960, 1962, 1963,
1971, and 1973 by The Lockman Foundation,
and are used by permission.

The use of selected references from various versions of the Bible in this publication does not
necessarily imply publisher endorsement of the
versions in their entirety.

Library of Congress Cataloging in Publication Data
Sanders, John Oswald, 1902-
  Prayer power unlimited.

  Includes bibliographical references and index.
  1. Prayer. I. Title.
BV210.2.S26   248'.3   77-23472
ISBN 0-8024-6808-X

Second Printing, 1978

Printed in the United States of America

Contents

Preface

The supreme importance of prayer is tacitly admitted by most evangelical Christians. It is accepted as an article of faith. And yet there are few areas of the Christian life in which there are more regretful confessions of failure and disappointment.

The author does not pose as an authority on the subject—only a fellow student in the school of prayer; he is very conscious of the heights yet to be scaled.

These chapters are the outcome of a series of studies on prayer delivered to a local congregation. The acceptance with which they met has encouraged their reproduction in this form.

It is not a book to be read through at a sitting. Its maximum value will be gained if the lessons are studied one at a time and put into practice in daily prayer. It could prove useful for home Bible study groups.

A prayer relating to the theme under consideration, from men of God in all ages, is given at the close of each chapter as an indication how others approach God. Discussion questions are also appended to each chapter.

Except where otherwise indicated, quotations are from the *New American Standard Bible*.

One Short Hour

Lord, what a change within us one short hour
Spent in Thy presence will prevail to make!
What heavy burdens from our bosoms take,
What parched grounds refresh as with a shower!
We kneel, and all around us seems to lower;
We rise, and all, the distant and the near,
Stands forth in sunny outline, brave and clear.
We kneel, how weak! we rise, how full of power!
Why, therefore, should we do ourselves this wrong,
Or others—that we are not always strong,
That we are ever overborne with care,
That we should ever weak or heartless be,
Anxious or troubled, when with us is prayer,
And joy and strength and courage are with Thee?

RICHARD CHENEVIX TRENCH

A School of Prayer

Lord, teach us to pray (Luke 11:1).

Do you long for a more satisfying prayer life? Are your prayers being answered? Are your prayers making an impact on the kingdom of darkness? If not, this book aims to throw a little light on some causes of failure and to suggest scriptural ways in which prayer can become more effective and satisfying—and more to God's glory.

Jesus had drawn His disciples apart for a quiet retreat, a rest from their arduous ministry. He took advantage of the seclusion to pray. His men were around Him. Whether He prayed audibly or not, we are not told. Perhaps they were privileged to listen, but in any case they watched Him at prayer. They saw His face rapt in devotion. They sensed the presence of God and were awed by it.

When He ceased praying, one of them (was it Peter?), doubtless voicing the desire of them all, said "Lord, teach us to pray just as John also taught his disciples" (Luke 11:1). They had seen His mighty miracles, but they did not ask for that power. They had heard His matchless preaching, but they did not ask Him to teach them how to preach. It was His prayer life, His communion with His Father, that they longed to know. He at

7

once responded to their request and proceeded to teach them to pray.

Is this not our paramount need too? Are we not conscious of the untapped possibilities of prayer? If Jesus responded so promptly to the plea of His apostles, will He be less willing to respond to our sincere desire, "Lord, teach us to pray?"

Are you willing to place yourself under His tuition? Will you enter what the saintly Andrew Murray called the "School of Prayer"? Are you prepared to master the lessons on prayer and work them out in practice? If you are willing, you can count on the utmost cooperation of the Holy Spirit, who is "the Spirit of grace and of supplication" (Zech 12:10).

The following chapters are based mainly on our Lord's teaching on prayer, although they are supplemented from other parts of Scripture. They may be regarded as separate lessons to be studied and then carried over into the daily life of prayer. We learn to pray only by praying, however well we may have mastered its theory.

Lord, teach us to pray.

1

Worship and Adoration

Worship the LORD *in the splendor of holiness*
(1 Chron 16:29, marg.).

A notable lesson in prayer was learned by the author when he read that in prayer there are at least five elements that should be present in a well-balanced prayer life. In a sense, prayer cannot be analyzed, since it is a unity and the outpouring of the single life of the one who prays. Yet in another sense, it can be divided into its constituent elements.

"The fact that [prayer] is worship, and the further fact that worship may be expressed in various forms," wrote H. W. Frost, "makes analysis possible. . . . Prayer is indeed one. But also it is multiform."[1]

The five enumerated elements are: worship, or adoration; thanksgiving; confession; petition; and intercession. This concept opened a new world of prayer, for hitherto his prayers had been almost entirely petition. Now the prayer life embraces whole new areas of spiritual experience.

Our Lord's immediate answer to the request of His disciples, "Lord, teach us to pray," was, "When you pray, say: 'Father'" (Luke 11:2). In other words, prayer begins with God. The pattern prayer He gave them was

9

halfway completed before He prayed for personal needs. The concerns and interests of God came first.

This is a supremely important lesson. If God is not given the chief place in our praying, our prayers will be anemic. When our thoughts begin with Him, love is kindled and faith stimulated. So our first lesson will be concerned with Him. We shall consider worship, or adoration, for this is involved in the petition "hallowed be Thy name" (v. 2).

Dr. R. A. Torrey, who was God's instrument to bring revival to many parts of the world, testified that an utter transformation came into his experience when he learned not only to pray and return thanks, but to worship—asking nothing from God, seeking nothing from Him, occupied with Himself, and satisfied with Himself.

The idea of worship is common to the whole human race. But as generally used, the word *worship* seldom conveys its full scriptural content. It means "to bow down or prostrate oneself." Worship is the adoring contemplation of God as He has revealed Himself in Christ and in the Scriptures. It is the act of paying honor and reverence to God. When we pray "hallowed be Thy name," we are worshipping Him.

F. W. Faber caught the sense of the word in these lines:

> How wonderful, how beautiful, the sight of Thee
>   must be,
> Thine endless wisdom, boundless power, and
>   awful purity.
> O how I fear Thee, living God, with deepest,
>   tenderest fears,
> And worship Thee with trembling hope, and
>   penitential tears.

The Old English form of the word, *worthship*, gives
an interesting sidelight on its meaning, implying worth-
iness on the part of the one who receives the honor. This
is reflected in the apocalyptic ascription of praise to
Christ: "Worthy is the Lamb that was slain to receive . . .
honor and glory and blessing" (Rev 5:12).

Worship flows from love, and where there is little love
there will be little worship. But there can be an element
of selfishness even in love. We can and should worship
God in gratitude for what He has done for us, but it
reaches a higher level when we worship Him simply for
what He is, for the perfections and excellences of His
own being.

"I have known men," said Thomas Goodwin, "who
came to God for nothing else but just to come to Him,
they so loved Him. They scorned to soil Him and themselves with any other errand than just purely to be alone
with Him in His presence."[2]

Worship, then, is the loving ascription of praise to
God for what He is, both in Himself and in His ways. It is
the bowing of the innermost spirit in deep humility and
reverence before Him.

When Scipio Africanus returned to Rome after a resounding victory, he rode in triumph, followed by his
captives. As he went, he scattered the largess of the
victor to the crowds that lined the way. Some were
stirred to gratitude by his liberality; some because he
had rolled away from their homes the fear of the invad-
ing army; still others, forgetful of their personal benefits, praised the qualities of the victor—his courage,
resourcefulness, liberality. It was in this last group that
the highest element of worship was present.

Worship can be wordless. "My soul, be thou silent
unto God," said the psalmist (Psalm 62:5, ASV, marg.).

There are times when words are an intrusion, times when the worshipper is hushed into awed silence by the ineffable Presence and can only be silent to God. A single word can enshrine a wealth of worship, as when the word *Rabboni* fell from Mary's lips (John 20:16).

But worship must be "in truth" (John 4:24, KJV), that is, free from mere profession or pretense. Brother Lawrence, that saint of the kitchen, learned that to worship God in truth is to acknowledge Him to be what He is, and to acknowledge ourselves to be what we are.

HOW WORSHIP IS STIMULATED

The scholar in the school of prayer may feel that God seems far away and unreal, so that attempts to worship Him seem a farce. The question arises, How can I know God better so that I can worship Him more worthily?

God has granted a partial revelation of Himself in the wonders of nature. "The heavens declare the glory of God" (Psalm 19:1, KJV). We learn there of His almighty power, His transcendent beauty, His unsearchable wisdom. But nature does not reveal Him as a God of love and mercy.

Only "in the face of Jesus Christ" will we see the full blaze of the divine glory (2 Cor 4:6, KJV). All the fullness of God dwells in Him in bodily form (Col 1:19), and no worship that ignores Christ is acceptable to God, for it is through Christ alone that we have access to the Father.

> In Thee, most perfectly expressed,
> The Father's glories shine,
> Of the full deity possessed,
> Eternally Divine!
> Worthy, O Lamb of God, art Thou,
> That ev'ry knee to Thee should bow.
>
> JOSIAH CONDOR

This raises a second question: How can I know Christ, who alone reveals God?

The answer is, of course, that we know Christ primarily through the Scriptures, which are the only tangible means of knowing Him. "You search the Scriptures, . . . and it is these that bear witness of Me" (John 5:39). In them is to be found the complete and satisfying interpretation of God in Christ.

The Scriptures are rich in material to feed and stimulate worship and adoration—especially the Psalms, which are God's inspired prayer book. As you read them, turn them into prayer. Vast tracts of truth await our exploration. Great themes abound—God's holiness, sovereignty, truth, wisdom, faithfulness, patience, love, mercy—all of which will call forth our worship.

The use of a good hymnbook in private devotions can be a great aid to worship. Not all of us find it easy to express our deepest feelings or to utter the love of our hearts to God. We are very conscious of the poverty of our thoughts of God and the inadequacy of the words in which we express them. But we can appropriate the outpouring of worship and praise of men and women whom the Spirit has gifted to express these thoughts in verse. Try using a hymnbook regularly.

We should guard against the idea that worship is confined to the realm of thought, for Scripture links worship with service. During the temptation in the wilderness, our Lord quoted the Old Testament: "You shall *worship* the Lord your God, and *serve* Him only" (Matt 4:10, italics added; cf. Deut 6:13, marg.). We should not separate what God has joined. Worship is no substitute for service, nor is service a substitute for worship. True worship will inevitably find expression in loving, sacrificial service.

PRAYER

Worthy of praise from every mouth,
   of confession from every tongue,
   of worship from every creature
Is Thy glorious Name, O Father, Son and Holy
Ghost;
   Who didst create the world in Thy grace
   and by Thy compassion didst save the world.
To Thy majesty, O God, ten thousand times ten
thousand
   bow down and adore,
Singing and praising without ceasing, and saying,
   Holy, holy, holy, Lord God of hosts;
Heaven and earth are full of Thy praises;
   Hosanna in the highest.

NESTORIAN LITURGY

QUESTIONS

1. What does it mean to "worship in spirit and truth" (John 4:24)?
2. Bishop Moule said, "Worship will be a powerful, secret means to our spiritual growth." In what ways will worship stimulate such growth?

2

Thanksgiving

Give thanks unto the LORD (Psalm 118:1, KJV).

The second element in prayer is thanksgiving, which is the glad and appreciative acknowledgment of the benefits and blessings God gives, either to ourselves or to others. It is an integral part of prayer, not an addendum to it.

Thanksgiving is to be distinguished from worship, for thanksgiving is not so much occupation with the perfections of God as it is the grateful acknowledgment of the love and kindness He has lavished on us. Worship easily and naturally leads us to thanksgiving, for God's perfections find expression in the daily gifts and blessings He gives.

Even if Scripture did not exhort us to give thanks always and for all things, common courtesy would accord a prominent place to thanksgiving in our prayer life, for we are constantly at the receiving end of God's generosity. Appreciation is the basis of healthy human relationships, and it is surely no less important in our relationship with God.

Aristotle called Memory the scribe of the soul, and it is good for us to let her do her work.

The Psalms abound in thanksgiving. "O give thanks unto the LORD" (Psalm 118:1, KJV). "Bless the LORD, O

JESUS GAVE THANKS

my soul, and forget none of His benefits" (Psalm 103:2). "Give thanks to the LORD, for He is good; for His lovingkindness is everlasting" (Psalm 118:1).

The prayers of our Lord were not lacking in this element. The occasions on which it is recorded that He gave thanks are significant but rather unexpected: At the grave of Lazarus (John 11:41); when He fed the five thousand (John 6:11); when the seventy returned with shouts of victory (Luke 10:21, KJV); when He instituted the Lord's Supper, giving thanks for the bitter cup He was to drink (Luke 22:19).

We too should call to mind the Lord's dealings with us—His mercies, which are new every morning (Lam 3:22-23), and the temporal gifts that recur with such regularity. We are unconscious of a great many of our blessings; they therefore go unacknowledged. "I have experienced today the most exquisite pleasure that I have ever had in my life," said a young invalid; "I was able to breathe freely for about five minutes."

Psalm 103 is a classic of worship blended with thanksgiving. A paraphrase by Dr. A. B. Bruce provides a model for our emulation.

> God is a beneficent Being. He delights to bestow penitence, He forgives sin, heals diseases, saves life, crowning His worshippers with garlands of love and mercy, and making their hearts young with gladness. He is a righteous God who espouses the cause of the oppressed and shields them from wrong; a magnanimous God, who bears patiently our shortcomings with a Father's heart, full of pity towards frail men, subject to infirmity and pain. He is mighty as well as merciful, sitting in majesty on His heavenly throne, and ruling as King over all receiving perfect obedience from the manifold powers of His universe, which do His will and show His glory.[1]

The psalmist's heart overflowed in thanksgiving and praise as he meditated on these themes, but he was conscious of the tendency that we know only too well—failure to give thanks for blessings received and prayers answered. So he apostrophizes his soul: "Bless the LORD, O my soul, and *forget none of His benefits*" (Psalm 103:2, italics added). We should have a definite time every day when we remember these with gratitude.

THANKFUL FOR EVERYTHING?

Thanksgiving is not difficult when it flows from our recognition of the temporal and spiritual blessings that we consider desirable. But what of the burdens and disciplines, the sufferings and sorrows of life? Surely we cannot be expected to give thanks for those! But this is exactly what God does expect us to do. We are left with no option if we are His obedient children. "In everything give thanks" (1 Thess 5:18, italics added). "*Always* giving thanks *for all things*" (Eph 5:20, italics added). These commands are devastatingly inclusive.

No one would suggest that this is always easy, but it is always possible, or God would not expect it of us. There is an Arab proverb that says, "All sunshine makes a desert," and it is true that if life were all joy and prosperity, unmixed with sorrow and adversity, our characters would be immeasurably the poorer. Our loving Father knows the exact proportions in which to mix these ingredients, and we should thankfully and without question accept His dealings with us as the very best for us.

The correct response of the heart is expressed in *The Scottish Prayer Book*: "We praise Thee for the grace by which Thou dost enable us so to bear the ills of the present world, that our souls are enriched by a fuller experience of Thy love, a more child-like dependence

on Thy will, and a deeper sympathy with the suffering
and the sad."

On His way to exile, Chrysostom exclaimed, "Thank
God for everything!" Thanking God in one of his
matchless letters, Samuel Rutherford wrote, "O, what I
owe to the furnace, the file and the hammer of my Lord
Jesus!"

A missionary was greatly discouraged. He knew that
his work was not progressing as it should. One day,
while visiting another missionary, he saw a motto card
on the wall: TRY THANKSGIVING! It was an arrow to
his soul. He suddenly realized that this element had
been largely missing from his prayers.

There had been plenty of asking God for things he
desired and needed; he had asked desperately at times,
but had forgotten to thank Him for what he received. He
began to count his blessings and to pour out his heart in
thanksgiving.

At once the power of the Spirit began to surge through
him, and the work at his missionary center began to
prosper. His lack of thanksgiving had been quenching
the working of the Holy Spirit. Have we been guilty of
the same sin?

The old couplet runs, "Prayers and praises go in pairs,
they have praises who have prayers," and this should be
true of us. John Newton, the converted slave-trader,
used to give thanksgiving a practical 'twist by saying
that true thanksgiving is thanksliving.

When we reach heaven and are in the immediate
presence of God, other aspects of prayer will cease, as
being no longer necessary or appropriate; but thanksgiving and worship will continue throughout eternity.

PRAYER

Father, with thankful and humble hearts we appear before Thee. We would thank Thee for all the benefits that we have received from Thy goodness. It is to Thy blessing that we owe what success we have found. Every opportunity for doing good, each victory we have gained over ourselves, every thought of Thy presence, are alike Thy gifts to us. The best thanksgiving we can offer Thee is to live according to Thy holy will.

MICHAEL SAILER

QUESTIONS

1. Is it possible to be genuinely thankful for everything? If so, in what sense?
2. What reflex blessing does thanksgiving bring to our lives?

3

Confession

I will confess my transgressions to the LORD (Psalm 32:5).

In considering our second lesson in the school of prayer, we reviewed thanksgiving and recalled the all too frequent times when we had failed to give God thanks. We have often deserved the rebuke that our Lord directed to the nine ungrateful lepers whom He had healed, but who failed to return to thank Him: "Were there not ten cleansed? But the nine—where are they?" (Luke 17:17).

Ingratitude is not an amiable infirmity but a sin. Shakespeare called it, "Ingratitude, thou marble-hearted fiend." "Unthankfulness is theft," said Luther. And we must all plead guilty to the charge in greater or less degree. And this sin and failure leads us to the theme of our third lesson.

We saw in the last chapter that the Psalms abound in thanksgiving, but they can be described with equal truth as the world's greatest confessional literature. "Is it surprising," asks A. Jean Courtney, "that the place where God is most praised should be where we read most about penitence? I suggest it is just what we might expect. The more we think of God's gifts, the smaller our own gifts to Him appear. No one suffers from self-righteousness who

spends much time in prayer."[1] Confession is the third
element in prayer.

The Greek word for *confession* means "to say the
same thing, to admit or declare oneself guilty of what
one is accused of." When I confess my sin to God, I am
agreeing with Him in His judgment of its guilt and
seriousness. I am viewing my sin from His perspective.
We talk the same language about it, and I take sides with
Him against it. Note the operative verbs in David's confession recorded in Psalm 32:1-5: "I acknowledged—I
did not hide—I will confess."

No confession that is not sincere and explicit will
either reach God's ear or quiet an accusing conscience.
This is made clear in 1 John 1:9: "If we confess our sins,
He is faithful and righteous to forgive us our sins and to
cleanse us from all unrighteousness." Our confession,
to be acceptable, must be not of sin in general, but of
sins—individual acts of sin.

There is a place for a general confession, for there are
many sins of which we are unconscious or which we
have overlooked; but this does not dispense with the
necessity for a frank and full confession of specific sins.
The confession should be made the moment we are
conscious of having sinned, and not delayed until a
more convenient time. We have the assurance that the
moment we sincerely confess, that moment God freely
forgives us and fellowship is restored.

The extent of confession poses a problem to some
sensitive and overscrupulous hearts. Is it sufficient to
make confession to God alone, or should we confess to
others or make public confession? The answer is that
there are three areas of confession that correspond to
three kinds of sin.

1. *Secret confession.* When the sin is against God

alone, then the confession need be to God alone. To confess to someone else would serve no purpose other than to give that person a knowledge of the sin, and there is no benefit in that.

2. *Private confession.* Some sins are against man as well as against God. The general principle is that the confession should be coextensive with the sin. Whenever possible, we should make confession to the offended party as well as to God.

The prodigal's sin was against his father as well as against his God. When he made confession, he rightly confessed: "I have sinned against heaven and in your sight" (Luke 15:21). Confession to God would have been inadequate and would not have brought peace of conscience; nor would it have restored him to the old filial relationship with his father. Once full confession was made, restoration was complete.

Our Lord gave clear instruction on this point. "If therefore you are presenting your offering at the altar, and there remember that your brother has something against you, leave your offering there before the altar, and go your way; first be reconciled to your brother, and then come and present your offering" (Matt 5:23-24). The order is: First go, then be reconciled, then come to present your gift.

3. *Public confession.* When the sin is public—against some group or church—the confession should be as public as was the sin. In this way the sin can be forgiven, confidence can be restored, and fellowship can be renewed. The very act of public confession would have a salutary effect that would be likely to deter a repetition of the sin.

There does not appear to be any scriptural warrant for the suggestion advanced in some circles that even secret sins should be publicly confessed. Where this has been done, much harm has sometimes resulted. As someone put it, although God knows all our thoughts and deeds, our fellowmen do not share His omniscience—nor need they. It is our social sins that we need to confess publicly, not our secret thoughts and secret acts of sin.

In times of revival, the confession of sins in public has sometimes occurred. But this has been the spontaneous, almost irresistible outpouring of a heart deeply convicted by the Holy Spirit. In these cases, the pressure of the Spirit on the heart is so strong that relief comes only with confession. But spontaneous confession under these circumstances and in the glow and warmth of a movement of the Spirit is a different thing from a confession that is not required by Scripture and not pressured by the Holy Spirit. These spontaneous confessions are extraordinary occasions and not the norm.

Contrition, or penitence, will accompany true confession. Contrition is such a deep grief of heart for sin that it becomes resolution to have done with that sin. Professed penitence without the purpose to forsake the sin confessed is insincere, and a mockery. Similarly, confession and professed contrition without a resulting change in life-style are without meaning and are unacceptable to God.

The depth of contrition and penitence of the prodigal son was seen in the confession and request he purposed to make of his father: "I am no longer worthy to be called your son; make me as one of your hired men" (Luke 15:19).

PRAYER

Most gracious, Almighty God, full of lovingkindness and longsuffering: we confess to Thee with our whole

heart our neglect and forgetfulness of Thy command-
ments, our wrong doing, and speaking and thinking, the
hurts we have done to others, and the good we have left
undone.

O Lord, blot out the transgressions that are against us,
for Thy goodness and Thy glory, and for the sake of Thy
Son, our Saviour, Jesus Christ.

ANONYMOUS

QUESTIONS

1. Is there a place for sharing the knowledge of some personal
   sin with a trusted friend and counselor?
2. What is the difference between the cleansing mentioned in
   1 John 1:7 and that in 1:9?

4

Petition and Intercession

Petitions, prayers, intercessions . . . for all men
(1 Tim 2:1, NEB).

In our fourth lesson, we turn from the Godward to the manward aspect of prayer—petition, when we are concerned about our own needs; and intercession, when we are concerned with the needs of others.

There are no fewer than twelve Hebrew words in the Old Testament and five Greek words in the New Testament that are translated "prayer." We are concerned with three of these New Testament words that are used by Paul in 1 Timothy 2:1 (NEB). "First of all, then, I urge that petitions, prayers, intercessions, and thanksgivings be offered for all men"—petitions, prayers, intercessions. Let us examine them more closely.

PETITIONS

This word *petition* is derived from the Greek word meaning "to beg, to lack." It can be and is used of both God and man. It refers here to petition for one's personal needs. The picture behind the word is that of a beggar sitting at the side of the road, begging the help of the king as he passes by. It expresses destitution and inadequacy; inability to meet one's own needs, and total dependence on another. It is need expressed in a cry.

27

When we come to God with our petitions, we come humbly and expectantly to the throne of grace, deserving nothing, but hoping in God's mercy. We respond to the gracious invitation: "Let us therefore draw near with confidence to the throne of grace, that we may receive mercy and may find grace to help in time of need" (Heb 4:16).

So *petitions* are pleas for the supply of a definite need keenly felt. It always has specific situations in view.

PRAYERS

The English word *prayers* in 1 Timothy 2:1 does not accurately or adequately reflect the meaning of its Greek equivalent. It is a more general term than *petitions*, and is used of God alone.

The Greek word is a combination of *pros*, "by the side of," and *euchomai*, "to wish." As used here, then, the word *prayers* means prayer-wishes that are expressed in the presence and by the side of another. The Other is, of course, our heavenly Father.

One good suggestion concerning the application of *prayers* is that the word refers to needs that are always present, in contrast to *petitions*, which have specific situations in view. For example, we offer *prayer* for the forgiveness only He can impart, or for the strength only He can give. The word is very wide in its meaning.

The word *prayers*, then, expresses the Spirit-begotten instinct to turn to God in every hour of need, and breathe out our prayer-wishes to Him, just as John's disciples did to Jesus (see Matt 14:12).

INTERCESSIONS

In petitions and prayers, we are concerned for ourselves and our own needs. In intercession, we are concerned for the needs and interests of others. Intercession is the unselfish and altruistic aspect of prayer.

The idea behind the Greek word is: "to fall in with a person, to draw near so as to converse freely, and hence to have freedom of access." It is the word used to describe a child who goes to its father in behalf of another, or a person who enters a king's presence to submit a petition.

In intercession, the believer is acting as an intermediary between God and man. He forgets himself and his own needs in his identification with the needs of the one for whom he prays. The prayers of Abraham for the people of Sodom (Gen 18:23-33) and of Moses for Israel (Ex 32:1-14) are classic examples of intercession.

In intercession there are reflex benefits to the one who prays, as well as direct benefits to the one for whom intercession is made. Henry Martyn observed that at times of inward dryness and depression he had often found a delightful revival in the act of praying for others' conversion or sanctification or prosperity in the work of the Lord. His dealings with God for them about these gifts and blessings were for himself a means of grace and blessing.

As we engage in this ministry, the thought of the intercession of our great High Priest is a source of comfort and stimulus. Lilias Trotter of North Africa told how the thought of Christ's intercession took on a new preciousness for her. She was reading of one to whom God had given a wonderful gift of prayer. The thought came to her, *O that we had someone among us who could pray like that!* And then, almost with the vividness of an audible voice, came the further thought, *Is not Jesus enough?*

In a later lesson this aspect of prayer is treated more fully.

PRACTICAL APPLICATION

In order that God's glory may be secured and the reader's prayer life enriched, it is suggested that he review his daily prayers, and so arrange them that each element—worship, thanksgiving, confession, petition, and intercession—finds a place. In the morning, perhaps, worship, petition, and intercession will have prominence; in the evening, confession, thanksgiving, and intercession.

PRAYER

We beseech Thee, Lord and Master, to be our help and succour. Save those among us who are in tribulation; have mercy on the lowly; lift up the fallen: show Thyself to the needy; heal the ungodly; convert the wanderers of Thy people; feed the hungry; raise up the weak; comfort the faint-hearted. Let all the people know that Thou art God alone, and Jesus Christ is Thy Son, and we Thy people and the sheep of Thy pasture.

CLEMENT OF ROME

QUESTIONS

1. God knows our needs before we ask Him. Why does He sometimes require us to keep on asking?
2. Does our intercession cause God to change His mind?

5

The Matchless Teacher

With strong crying and tears (Heb 5:7, KJV).

Our most wonderful lesson and our greatest inspiration in the holy art of prayer come from Him who not only spoke as never man spoke, but prayed as never man prayed. It is Luke who especially captures for us the teaching and habits of prayer in the life of our Lord.

We are inclined to think, are we not, that the human needs of our Lord were less real and pressing than our own, and that somehow His human nature was aided and sustained by His divine nature in a way that ours cannot be. Consequently, it is easy to feel that His need of prayer was surely not so desperate as ours.

But a moment's thought will correct this misconception. Did His deity lessen the intensity of His anguish in the Garden of Gethsemane? Did it banish His hunger or dispel His weariness? The whole testimony of the gospels leads to the view that His deity in no way affected the reality of His human nature. The only difference is that He did no sin. His prayers were as real and intense as those of any other man.

This will be borne out by a study of His prayer life, and it is suggested that the reader make this a special study. So completely did He renounce the independent exercise of His divine powers and prerogatives that, like the

weakest of His followers, He became dependent on His
Father for all. Just as we do, He received His daily and
hourly needs through the medium of prayer.

> Why need He pray, who held by filial right,
> O'er all the world alike of thought and sense,
> The fulness of his Sire's omnipotence?
> Why crave in prayer what was his own by might?
>
> Vain is the question,—Christ was man in need,
> And being man his duty was to pray.
> The son of God confess'd the human need,
> And doubtless ask'd a blessing every day.
> Nor ceases yet for sinful man to plead,
> Nor will, till heaven and earth shall pass away.
>
> HARTLEY COLERIDGE

WHERE DID HE PRAY?

He prayed in solitude. If "prayer is the Christian's
vital breath, the Christian's native air," it was no less so
to his Lord. It was the natural atmosphere of His life.
Whenever possible, He sought solitude so that He could
commune with His Father. It has been remarked that
there are three kinds of solitude—the solitude of time,
the solitude of place, and the solitude of spirit. Jesus
experienced all of these.

Robert E. Speer notes that one of His two prayers of
deepest power was offered before midnight at the Tem-
ple gates (John 17), the other just after midnight in
Gethsemane (Matt 26:36). He used to spend whole
nights in prayer (Luke 6:12), and would rise to pray long
before sunrise (Mark 1:35).

He also chose secluded places so that He, sometimes
with His disciples, could pray undisturbed. The mountains, the desert, a garden were His favorite haunts (Matt
14:13, 23; Mark 6:46; Luke 5:16; 6:12; John 18:2).

Even in the midst of crowds He experienced a solitude of spirit. Consider the paradoxical statement of Luke 9:18: "And it came about that while He was praying alone, the disciples were with Him." He apparently possessed such powers of concentration and abstraction that He did not allow even the presence of His friends to disturb the solitude of His spirit. His longest recorded prayer was prayed in the presence of others (John 17).

He prayed in different attitudes. While posture is secondary to attitude of spirit, it is instructive to note that at times Jesus prayed when standing, just where He happened to be at the moment (Matt 14:19; John 11:41). At another time He knelt (Luke 22:41). On yet another occasion He fell on His face (Matt 26:39). We might well ask: "If the Son of God got down upon His knees and at times fell on His face before God, what attitude should we ordinary mortals assume as we enter the divine presence?"

He prayed in secret. Much of His prayer life was concealed even from His intimates. His own practice was reflected in His command to His disciples: "When you pray, go into your inner room, and when you have shut your door, pray to your Father who is in secret" (Matt 6:6). Shut in with God, shut out from all else. He taught them that secret prayer brought open reward. "Thy Father which seeth in secret shall reward thee" (v. 6, KJV). Near the close of His ministry, these poignant words occur: "And everyone went to his home. But Jesus went to the Mount of Olives" (John 7:53—8:1)— probably to spend the night in secret vigil.

> How oft He sought the mountain top, and
>   knelt upon its crest,
> To pray, and lay His weary Head upon
>   His Father's breast.

Before He called the Twelve to Him, He prayed
    all night alone,
And when the day began to dawn, He chose
    them for His own.
                    GREAT COMMISSION PRAYER LEAGUE

WHEN DID HE PRAY?

He prayed in the morning, at the gateway of the day
(Mark 1:35). He prayed in the evening, when the day's
work was over (Mark 6:46).

Great crises were preceded by prayer. It was "while
He was praying" *at His baptism* that heaven was opened
and the Holy Spirit descended on Him (Luke 3:21-22).
This was the watershed of His life and ministry, for He
was identifying Himself with the godly remnant of the
apostate nation.

He prayed *in the hour of His popularity,* the time
when so many are swept off their feet. When great
crowds were thronging Him, "He Himself would often
slip away to the wilderness and pray" (Luke 5:16). The
glamour of popular approval never carried Him away,
for He was fortified by prayer.

His *selection of the twelve apostles,* a seemingly un-
important yet in reality epoch-making event in world
history, was made only after a night of prayer (Luke
6:12-13). To them He was to commit the responsibility
of carrying His Gospel to the ends of the earth.

It was after a special time of prayer that He opened His
heart to His disciples and shared with them the dread
fact of His *approaching suffering and death* (Luke 9:18,
21-22).

It was while He was in the act of prayer that the
majestic *transfiguration scene* was enacted, when "the
appearance of His face became different, and His cloth-

ing became white and gleaming," and the approving and authenticating voice of the Father was heard (Luke 9:29, 35). Prayer was the cause, transfiguration was the effect. Is there a lesson here for us?

Great achievements were preceded by prayer. Many of His miracles followed prayer: the feeding of the four thousand (Matt 15:36); the feeding of the five thousand (John 6:11); walking on the water (Matt 14:23-33); the raising of Lazarus (John 11:41-42); the healing of the insane boy (Mark 9:14-29). Each of these miracles was linked with the prayer that preceded it, and this is probably true of His other miracles.

Great achievements were followed by prayer. When confronted with great crises or with demanding tasks, we turn instinctively to prayer. But once the crisis is over, the task achieved, we tend to lean again on our own abilities or wisdom. Jesus guarded against this evil by following such occasions with prayer, and we would do well to imitate our divine Exemplar. After what had been perhaps one of His most successful days, instead of courting the popularity of the crowd, He dismissed them and sought solitude for prayer (Matt 14:23).

Great pressure of work was a call to prayer. Our Lord's life was exceptionally busy. He worked under constant pressure. At times He had no leisure even for meals (Mark 6:31). But whatever the pressure, He made sure that prayer did not become a casualty. To Him it was a call to devote extra time to prayer (Mark 1:32-35; Luke 5:15-16; John 6:15).

Great sorrows were faced with prayer. The Man of sorrows suffered deeply at the hands of His own people. Added to this was the disappointment of His intimate followers' chronic lack of insight and understanding. But the darkest abyss was being forsaken by His Father

when Jesus assumed the sins of the whole world. For
this He fortified Himself in prayer (Matt 26:36-46).
He died praying. The hour and suffering of death were
powerless to quench the habit of a lifetime. His last
utterance was one of trustful prayer (Luke 23:46).

HOW DID HE PRAY?

A large field may be seen through a small chink in the
fence. While it is true that only a small segment of our
Lord's life is preserved for us in the gospels, what is
recorded by inspiration of the Spirit has been carefully
selected and may be regarded as representative. His
recorded prayers, therefore, afford a rich insight into His
heart and provide much material for emulation.

His Father's glory was His consuming passion. He
summarized His life's work in seven words: "I have
glorified thee on the earth" (John 17:4, KJV). This was
the focus of His prayer life. He secured God's glory by
completing the task entrusted to Him.

Thanksgiving was intermingled with worship and
petition. Adoring thankfulness constantly welled up in
His heart. Whether He was walking in bright sunlight or
in dark shadow, He did not forget thanksgiving.

Confession of sin found no place in His devotional
life, as it must in ours. This was because there was never
any consciousness of defilement or sense of distance
from His Father. On the contrary, He asserted, "I always
do the things that are pleasing to Him" (John 8:29). No
occasion for confession ever arose.

Communion with His Father bulked large in His
prayers, whereas petition for personal needs occupied
only a minor place. Amid earth's pollution, He pined for
the celestial air. His high-priestly prayer recorded in

John 17 is an example of communion with God at its highest.

Intercession also held an important place, and included the interests and spiritual advancement of His disciples. His prayer for Peter opens a wonderful line of truth: "Simon, Simon, behold, Satan has demanded permission to sift you [plural, 'you all'] like wheat; but I have prayed for you [singular]" (Luke 22:31-32). He prayed for His enemies, even for those who crucified Him (Luke 23:34).

His prayers were invariably answered. "I knew that Thou hearest Me always," was His testimony (John 11:42). This assurance rested on the fact that He knew He always prayed in line with the will of God.

From the gospel records it seems clear that of all His excellences of character, it was His prayerfulness that most impressed His apostles.

"The Lord Jesus is still praying," wrote S. D. Gordon. "Thirty years of living; thirty years of serving; one tremendous act of dying; nineteen hundred years of prayer. What an emphasis on prayer!"[1]

PRAYER

Blessed Lord, in lowly adoration I would bow before Thee. Thy whole redemption work has now passed into prayer: all that now occupies Thee in maintaining and dispensing what Thou didst purchase with Thy blood is only prayer. Thou ever livest to pray. And because we are, and abide in Thee, direct access to the Father is always open, our life can be one of unceasing prayer, and the answer to our prayer is sure.

ANONYMOUS

QUESTIONS

1. Write down definite ways in which it is possible for you to follow the example of the Master in prayer.
2. Since Jesus was never out of touch with His Father, why do you think He found prayer so necessary?

6

Pleading the Promises

His precious and magnificent promises (2 Pet 1:4)

The original owners of the fabulous Mt. Morgan gold mine in Queensland, Australia, toiled for many years on its barren slopes, eking out a frugal living, unaware that beneath their feet lay one of the richest mountains of gold the world has ever known. Their potential wealth was incalculable, but they lived on the bread line—all because they were ignorant of the wealth they possessed. The same is true of many Christians. In the promises of Scripture we have "unsearchable riches" (Eph 3:8, KJV); but because we fail to appropriate them, we live in comparative spiritual poverty. This is the subject of our next lesson.

"Every promise of Scripture is a writing of God," said Charles Haddon Spurgeon, "which may be pleaded before Him with this reasonable request, 'Do as Thou hast said.' The Creator will not cheat the creature who depends upon His truth; and far more, the heavenly Father will not break His word to His own child."[1]

WHAT IS A PROMISE?

A promise is a written or verbal declaration that binds the person who makes it to do or forbear a specified act.

39

When used of God, it is His pledge or undertaking to do
or refrain from doing a certain thing. Such promises
form the basis of the prayer of faith. It is through prayer
that these promises are turned into the facts and factors
of one's Christian experience.

The validity and dependability of a promise rest on
the character and resources of the one who makes it, just
as the validity of a bank check depends on the probity
and bank balance of the one who signs it. The holy
character and faithfulness of God make His promises
credible. "He who promised is faithful," testified the
writer of the letter to the Hebrews (10:23). "Not one
word has failed of all His good promise," said the kneeling Solomon (1 Kings 8:56).

God's promises are thus bound up with His character,
and rest on four of His divine attributes: (1) His *truth*,
which makes lying impossible; (2) His *omniscience*,
which makes His being deceived or mistaken impossible; (3) His *power*, which makes everything possible,
and (4) His *unchangeableness*, which precludes vacilla-
tion or change.

So when we come to God armed with one of His
promises, we can do so with the utmost confidence. We
can share Abraham's unstaggering trust. "With respect
to the promise of God, he did not waver in unbelief, but
grew strong in faith, giving glory to God, and being fully
assured that what He had promised, He was able also to
perform" (Rom 4:20-21).

THE RANGE OF THE PROMISES

One of the astonishing features of the Bible is the wide
range and variety of the promises it contains. Peter calls
them "His precious and magnificent promises" (2 Pet

1:4). Some diligent but anonymous Bible student claimed that there are no fewer than thirty thousand such promises awaiting appropriation. Whether this claim is true or not, it is certain that the larger proportion of these verses relate to prayer.

It is worthy of note that all the universal terms of the English language—*whatever, whenever, wherever, whoever, all, any, every*—are repeatedly used in connection with prayer, as though to encourage one's timid faith. In your reading, watch out for these inclusive and expansive words.

God's promises thus cover the whole range of human need. There will be no conceivable circumstances of life for which there is not an appropriate promise waiting to be claimed. They are keys that will open every lock, for they cover the whole realm of human experience.

> There are heights of sweet communion that are
> awaiting me,
> There are ocean depths of mercy that are flowing
> full and free;
> There are precious pearls of promise that can
> ne'er be priced in gold,
> There's a fulness in my Saviour that has
> never yet been told.

J. Stuart Holden

When reading Scripture, we should be alert to discover what God has promised to do, and then we should lay hold of His promise. "The man who desires to have power with God and prevail, cannot make too sure of the pleas and promises which undergird his supplications."[2]

We shall discover promises for adversity and prosperity; promises of peace, guidance, protection, strength,

deliverance, joy, and a hundred other blessings. John
Bunyan made the intriguing comment that the stepping
stones of Scripture run through every Slough of De-
spond.

But there is a yawning gap between the vast range of
God's promises and our experience of their fulfillment
simply because we have not bestirred ourselves to claim
them. Are we claiming our inheritance? God assures us
that we are "heirs according to the promise" (Gal 3:29,
KJV).

Think of the blessings assured in some of the great
prayer promises. (1) Anything is possible that is within
the will of God. "All things are possible to him who
believes" (Mark 9:23). (2) Adequate grace is available for
every need. "My God shall supply all your needs" (Phil
4:19). (3) Immediate help is assured in time of need.
"Before they call, I will answer; and while they are still
speaking, I will hear (Isa 65:24). (4) The limitless ability
of God is at our disposal. He "is able to do exceeding
abundantly beyond all that we ask or think" (Eph 3:20).
(5) Tranquility flows from prayer. "In everything by
prayer and supplication . . . and the peace of God, which
surpasses all comprehension, shall guard your hearts
and your minds in Christ Jesus" (Phil 4:6-7).

We are not authorized to claim in prayer things that
God has not promised. This seeming restriction is
greatly offset by the variety and comprehensiveness of
the promises. We should therefore make sure that our
petitions come within the scope of what has been offered. James and John, in asking the Lord to grant them
places of honor on either side of Him, were asking for
something for which they had no warrant, and their
request was not granted (Mark 10:35-40).

TURNING PROMISES INTO FACTS

In the practice of prayer, it is important to distinguish between promises and facts. They may often look alike, but a more careful reading will reveal an important difference. In spiritual experience, the distinction is much more than academic. Indeed, it can prove life-transforming.

We are to believe and accept as true every revealed fact of God's Word.

We are to plead and claim the fulfillment of every promise of God's Word.

If there is a clear statement of fact, faith accepts it without question. If there is a promise, faith fulfills any conditions that are attached and then pleads it in full confidence of its being fulfilled.

A fact calls forth our praise.

A promise calls for our claiming.

The function of faith is to turn God's promises into facts. Let us consider two examples.

"Where two or three have gathered together in My name, *there I am* in their midst" (Matt 18:20, italics added). Is this a promise or a fact? It is usually treated as though it were the former. Actually, it is not a promise for us to claim, but a simple assertion of fact. Jesus said, "There *I am*," not "There *I will be* if you claim My promise." What point is there in pleading with Christ to be present when He says He is already there?

"God . . . *has blessed us* with every spiritual blessing in the heavenly places in Christ" (Eph 1:3, italics added). Promise or fact? Paul does not say that God will bless us *if* we lay hold of the promise, but He asserts that God *has already* blessed us, and we have simply to believe it and enjoy the reality of it in our experience.

Seeing the terrible aftermath of violence and suffering that followed Cambodia's fall to the Khmer Rouge in 1975, a magazine writer asked: "How does one relate this tragedy with God's promise that when He opens a door, no man is able to shut it? Has God failed?"

The answer is twofold. (1) The text quoted, "Behold, I put before you an open door which no one can shut" (Rev 3:8), is not a promise, but a statement of fact. There is therefore no question of God's failing to keep His promise. (2) In the previous verse, the Lord had said that He is the One who "opens and no one will shut, *and who shuts and no one opens*" (italics added). Although no one can shut a door that God has opened (v. 8), He reserves the sovereign right to shut a door Himself when His purpose has been fulfilled (v. 7), and He did so in the case of Cambodia. The problem is solved when a statement of fact is differentiated from a promise.

But because He shut the door, does that mean that His purposes for Cambodia had failed? Despite the tragedy, within a few weeks of Cambodia's fall this report was received:

> Jimmy Rim, a Korean, reports that 600 Cambodians have turned to Christ in a refugee camp in Thailand. In northeast Thailand John Ellison has led over 100 refugees to Christ. Norman and Marie Ens saw 21 come to Christ recently in Bangkok. Merle Graven spoke in the Indiantown Gap Refugee Centre, and 123 Cambodians responded to the invitation. At Camp Pendleton 118 persons have accepted Christ. Andrew Way of OMF is training 170 for baptism in South Thailand. Within a period of approximately three months, about 1000 Cambodian refugees have accepted Christ.[3]

The significance of all this will be seen when it is

remembered that five years ago there were only six hundred Christians in Cambodia.

PROMISES MUST BE CLAIMED

The promises of God must be claimed in faith. It was "by faith" that the patriarchs "obtained promises" (Heb 11:33). In many cases there is a condition attached to the promise. Our part is to fulfill the condition, claim the answer, and confidently wait for it. It is here that we often have to do battle with our adversary the devil. Faith is always tested, and he will do all in his power to dislodge us from the plane of faith. "Satan comes and takes away the word" (Mark 4:15).

John Bunyan graphically described his experience as he endeavored to claim the promises. "Satan· would labour to pull the promise from me, telling me that Christ did not mean me in John 6:37. He pulled, and I pulled. But God be praised, I got the better of him."

OUR ATTITUDE TO THE PROMISES

We can adopt one of three attitudes to God's promises.

1. We can *"come short"* of them by devaluing them to the level of our past experience (Rom 3:23, KJV). It is possible for us so to tone them down that we come far short of what God is offering us.

2. We can *"stagger"* or *"waver"* in unbelief because the risk involved seems too great or because the promise seems too good to be true (Rom 4:20; see also KJV). But he who wavers misses the blessing.

3. We can be *"fully assured,"* and *receive* the promises. Abraham, the man of faith was "fully assured that what He had promised, He was able also to perform" (Rom 4:21).

> The Lord has promised good to me,
> His Word my hope secures;
> IIe will my shield and portion be
> As long as life endures.
>
> JOHN NEWTON

With God, promise and performance are inseparable. "For as many as may be the promises of God, in Him they are yes; wherefore also by Him is our Amen to the glory of God through us" (2 Cor 1:20).

When God makes a promise, that promise is His yes, and Jesus is the guarantee of its fulfillment. The yes is God's. "Amen" is my response of faith—my expression of confidence that the promise will be fulfilled. I say amen in this sense when I cash a check signed by another person.

It is a poor compliment if we respond to God's gracious yes with a faltering amen.

PRAYER

O Lord Jesus Christ, who hast said that Thou art the way, the truth and the life; suffer us not at any time to stray from Thee, who art the way; nor to distrust the promises, who art the truth; nor to rest in any other thing but Thee, who art the life; beyond which there is nothing to be desired, neither in heaven nor on earth; for Thy Name's sake.

ERASMUS

QUESTIONS

1. Go through one of the briefer epistles and distinguish the promises from the facts in it.
2. What is taught concerning the relationship of God to His promises in the following Scriptures: Psalm 105:42; Romans 4:21; Hebrews 10:23; 2 Peter 3:9.

7

Discovering the Will of God

The will of God . . . good . . . acceptable . . . perfect
(Rom 12:2).

Our seventh lesson centers on John's confident statement: "And this is the confidence which we have before Him, that, if we ask anything according to His will, He hears us. And if we know that He hears us in whatever we ask, we know that we have the requests which we have asked from Him" (1 John 5:14-15).

In this passage, God binds Himself to answer every prayer that comes within the scope of His will. The implications of this statement are breathtaking. Our wonder deepens when we remember that God's will is always "good and acceptable and perfect" (Rom 12:2).

But there are negative implications as well. The clause "according to His will" places a very definite limitation on the assurance of an answer. Before we endeavor to learn how to discover God's will, let us consider the will of God itself.

WHAT IS THE WILL OF GOD?

God's will is what He sovereignly purposes and plans, and as such it cannot be improved. It is perfect. Paul says that it is also "good and acceptable," but not every

believer finds it easy to agree with him. The problem
arises from our innate tendency to characterize what is
good mainly in terms of creature comfort. We consider
God's will to be good when it means exemption from
trouble and pain, from sorrow and poverty, from bereavement and ill-health; and when it makes provision
for a modicum of luxury.

But such a concept finds little support in the New
Testament; rather, the reverse is stated. What does Paul
consider to be good? The answer is given in Romans
8:28-29: "And we know that God causes all things to
work together for good to those who love God, to those
who are called according to His purpose. For whom He
foreknew, He also predestined *to become conformed to
the image of His Son*" (italics added).

This often misinterpreted passage clearly teaches that
anything that makes us more like Christ is good. Christ-
likeness does not always thrive best in trouble-free conditions. It is more often the adverse conditions we face
that most effect the transformation.

So when we "ask anything according to His will," we
are really asking for what is the very best for us. The
corollary is that our requests are denied only when they
are against our highest interests. And would I not deny
my little boy's request for a sharp razor-blade, however
much he cries for it? So this apparent limitation to
answered prayer is in effect a gracious act of love.

HOW CAN WE KNOW GOD'S WILL?

We face a dual problem. How can we know with
certainty what is, and what is not, the will of God? If I do
not know with certainty that my petition is in the will of
God, how can I pray in faith? There must be a reasonable
and satisfying answer, or God could be charged with

unfairness in imposing a condition we are unable to fulfill.

It is the writer's conviction that the answer to our questions will gradually emerge as we engage in the practice of prayer, rather than while we are studying its theory. Study is, of course, necessary, but it must not be divorced from actual praying.

True prayer is not asking God for what *we* want, but for what *He* wants. This is implicit in the petition of the pattern prayer: "Thy will be done in earth" (Matt 6:10, KJV, italics added); and as William Barclay remarks, it is not "Thy will be changed," but "Thy will be done." Prayer is not a convenient method of getting one's own way or of bending God to one's desires.

Prayer is the means by which our desires can be redirected and aligned with the will of God. As we expectantly pray for light concerning the will of God on any matter, if our desires are not in line with His will, He will make it clear. If we are willing, He will change and redirect our desires, as Paul assures us: "It is God who is at work in you, both to will and to work for His good pleasure" (Phil 2:13).

We must not imagine that God will indiscriminately grant anything we desire. What would happen in the world if this were the case? What chaos! The farmer prays urgently for rain to save his crops on the same day that the vacationist earnestly prays for sunshine. People in Britain pray in time of war for the success of their armies, while the Germans are praying for victory for their troops. God cannot grant both requests.

How are we to pray in such situations? Only one prayer is appropriate: "Lord, we do not know what to pray for as we ought; may Thy will be done on earth in this matter as it is done in heaven" (see Romans 8:26 and Matt 6:10).

The supreme example of the redirection of the will in prayer is that of our Lord in Gethsemane's garden. As Son of Man, Jesus was utterly submissive to His Father's will. Yet in His humanity He shrank from the unutterable sufferings involved in His work as Mediator. In His distress He prayed, "Father, if Thou art willing, remove this cup from Me; yet not My will, but Thine be done" (Luke 22:42). Had He been certain that it was the will of His Father to accept that cup, His prayer would have been pointless. But He was not certain, and prayed to discover His Father's will, and the answer came.

In this petition we come face to face with the mystery of Christ's two natures. Note the "My will" and "Thy will." As Man, He longed to be spared the agony ahead; but as He prayed, the mists surrounding His Father's will were dissolved, and the issues became clear. He embraced His Father's will, His human will became merged with it, and He delighted in it.

His second prayer had no, "My will" and "Thy will" in it. In Matthew 26:42 it is simply, "Thy will be done." Then He "prayed a third time, saying the same thing once more" (Matt 26:44). And what was the outcome of the three sessions of prayer? Did He induce the Father to change His mind and remove the cup? No, indeed. But in prayer the will of God became clear, and Jesus was led to accept it with exultation. Listen to the joy and the inflexible purpose of His redirected will as He speaks to Peter: "The cup which the Father has given Me, shall I not drink it?" (John 18:11).

Amy Wilson Carmichael, founder of the Dohnavur Fellowship in India, said that early in their work they decided that before asking for anything, they should find out whether it was the mind of the Lord, although that kind of praying took time. The more they searched the Scriptures, the more they were encouraged to ask to be filled with the knowledge of His will before offering petitions for a desired benefit.

The experience of Christ in Gethsemane teaches us that prayer is not necessarily unanswered when it is not answered exactly as we would wish. It is clearly stated that the Lord's prayers were answered: "In the days of His flesh, He offered up both prayers and supplications with loud crying and tears to the One able to save Him from death, and He was heard because of His piety" (Heb 5:7).

The answer was not what His human nature craved, but through prayers and tears He was brought to the place where He preferred and chose His Father's will, and proved it to be "good and acceptable and perfect" (Rom 12:2). In our experience, as in His, sometimes it is only through tears and heartbreak that we reach the place where we can say with all our hearts, "Even so, Father: for so it seemed good in thy sight" (Matt 11:26, KJV).

In His high-priestly prayer, however, the emphasis is different. Then He knew with full assurance that His petition was in keeping with His Father's will. He did not say, "Father, if Thou art willing" (Luke 22:42). Instead, He boldly prayed, "Father, I will that they also, whom thou hast given me, be with me where I am" (John 17:24, KJV, italics added). In matters in which the will of God is clear, we can ask with complete confidence of a full answer.

How then are we to discern the will of God in specific matters so that we can offer the prayer of faith?

1. Let us recognize that *all matters of moral and spiritual principle are clearly dealt with in the Scriptures.* In studying them, we can find in general God's will on matters of moment in our daily lives. For example, God speaks clearly on matters of morals, the marriage relationship, relationship with others, ethical behavior, social responsibility, and so on. It is our responsibility to search out what is revealed. Where the Scriptures speak clearly, we need seek no further guidance. So the first question to ask is, Is what I am asking something that is sanctioned by the Word of God?

2. In applying general principles to specific cases for which there is no clear biblical guidance, we are to *look to the Holy Spirit to teach us.* It is axiomatic that He will never guide us to ask something that is contrary to the Scriptures He has inspired. But as we pray, sincerely seeking and choosing God's will, He will restrain us from offering petitions that are not acceptable. Or, on the other hand, He will impart a deepening assurance of what is God's will in the matter. This inner assurance then becomes the basis for the prayer of faith.

3. If we are sure our prayers are moving in the direction of God's will, we can expect Him to *add confirmation by giving indications of the divine providence in the circumstances.*

A helpful example of this principle is given in the experience of Paul and his companions on the fateful missionary journey that brought them to Macedonia (Acts 16:6-10). After being twice restrained by the Holy Spirit from proceeding in a direction that was not in His plan for them, they spent some time at Troas, where they waited on God to discover His will. Since Mysia and Bithynia had both proved to be out of God's will, what were they to do?

God answered their earnest and submissive prayers by granting them a vision which was confirmed by the Holy Spirit. Luke records their reaction: "Immediately we sought to go into Macedonia, concluding [assuredly gathering, KJV] that God had called us to preach the gospel to them" (v. 10). As the missionaries moved forward in this confidence, circumstances confirmed that in their prayer they had correctly discerned the will of God.

4. Another way God indicates His will is in *laying on our hearts a special burden* for someone or some situation, from which we can find relief only in prayer. When this occurs, we may conclude that He has so burdened us because He intends to work through our prayers. He thus takes us into fellowship with himself in the ministry of intercession.

Thomas Goodwin, the Puritan, wrote in this connection: "The Holy Spirit who is the Intercessor within us, and who searches the deep things of God, doth offer, prompt and suggest to us in our prayers those very things that are in God's heart, to grant the thing we desire of Him, so as it often comes to pass that a poor creature is carried on to speak God's very heart to Himself, and then God cannot, nor doth not deny."[1]

PRAYER

Set before our minds and hearts, O heavenly Father, the example of our Lord Jesus Christ, who when He was upon earth, found His refinement in doing the will of Him who sent Him, and in finishing His work. Give us grace to remember Him who knew neither impatience of spirit nor confusion of work, but in the midst of all His labours held communion with Thee, and even upon

earth was still in heaven; where now He reigneth with
Thee and the Holy Spirit, world without end.

DEAN C. J. VAUGHAN

QUESTIONS

1. Could God retain His sovereignty if He dispensed with this
   condition of answered prayer?
2. Does praying in submission to the will of God hinder us
   from praying the prayer of faith?

8

The All-Powerful Name

Anything in My name (John 14:14).

Is it not significant that in His last discourse with His disciples, our Lord six times in close succession spoke of praying "in My name" (John 14:13-14; 15:16; 16:23-27)? He must surely have attached singular importance to this advanced lesson in the school of prayer.

It is the view of Dr. A. T. Pierson that this truth of identity with Christ in the use of His name is the richest lesson ever taught even by the Lord Himself, and this is the theme of our eighth study.

It was a new concept to the apostles, and He endeavored to impress them with the all-prevailing power He was placing in their hands. "Until now you have asked for nothing in My name," He said; "ask, and you will receive, that your joy may be made full" (John 16:24). Henceforth their prayers were to have a new dimension and they were to pray in a different way. As they prayed in His name, the Father would hear and answer their prayers for His sake.

In encouraging the disciples so to pray, He used universal and unconditional terms concerning the level of answer they could expect — *whatever, anything* — so influential is the name of Christ. As Samuel Chadwick wrote, "Prayer reaches its highest level when offered in the Name which is above every name, for it lifts the petitioner into unity and identity with Himself."[1]

PRAYING IN THE NAME

What does it mean to pray in the name of Christ? It is a striking fact that Jesus never defined what He meant by this — apparently because it would be self-evident to members of the nation to which God had entrusted the honor of His name. This is implicit, for example, in God's lament: "My holy Name, which you have profaned among the nations where you went" (Ezek 36:22).

The name stands for the person. When a name is called, we immediately envisage the person bearing it. When Jesus said to His Father, "I manifested Thy name to the men whom Thou gavest Me" (John 17:6), He meant that He had shown them God's character, all that He is in Himself and in His relations to men. To believe "in the name of the only begotten Son of God" (John 3:18) means to believe in the person of Christ, in all that He is and has done. The name stands for the person.

In this connection, Dr. H. W. Frost makes an illuminating comment.

> First, a name signifies personality, for names are given to distinguish between individuals. . . . Second, a name signifies a person's character, for the name which designates a person stands for what that person is. . . . Third, a name signifies a person's life-work, or life-history, for . . . what he is represents also what he has done. . . . Fourth, a name signifies a person's reputation before men. . . . [Fifth] . . . , a person's name signifies the individual's standing before God, for . . . [it] represents . . . what he has done.[2]

Bearing these thoughts in mind, we note that the significance of the name of our Lord lies, in part, in the fact that in Scripture there are no fewer than 143 names and titles given to Him, each of which reflects light on His character and work. His is indeed a name above every name.

Is it not a staggering thought that our unique and glorious Lord has authorized us to make use of His mighty name in our prayers? There is obviously infinitely greater significance in this than merely appending the formula "in Jesus' name" to our prayers, for His name enshrines not only His love but also His power.

MAKING USE OF HIS NAME

What does it mean to do something in the name of another? Does it not imply that we do it as his representative and with his power and authority? We are not acting in our own name or authority. The Pharisee in Christ's parable came to God in his own name and pleaded his own virtues, and he went away empty (Luke 18:9-14). We have been authorized to make Christ's name the basis of our plea. Our prayers are answered and we experience God's favor on the grounds of His merit, not our own.

A striking example of the use of another's name occurs in Esther 8:7-8. "So King Ahasuerus said to Queen Esther and to Mordecai . . . 'Write to the Jews as you see fit, in the king's name, and seal it with the king's signet ring; for a decree which is written in the name of the king and sealed with the king's signet ring may not be revoked.'" Is this not exactly what Christ is doing? He entrusts us with His name and gives us the signet ring of God so that what we ask in His name becomes divinely authoritative.

So when we pray in His name, it means that we present prayers that He can endorse and of which He would approve. We shall pray only for things that are consistent with His name and character.

A man entrusts his loved wife, who is one with him in interests and purpose, with his check book, but he would not entrust it to an embezzler. So Christ entrusts the use of His name to those who are in harmony with Him in His purpose and who have a community of interest with Him in seeking His Father's glory.

"To pray in the Name of Christ," said Samuel Chadwick, "is to pray as one who is at one with Christ, whose mind is the mind of Christ, whose desires are the desires of Christ, and whose purpose is one with that of Christ. . . . Prayers offered in the Name of Christ are scrutinised and sanctified by His nature, His purpose, and His will. Prayer is endorsed by the Name, when it is in harmony with the character, mind, desire, and purpose of the Name."[3]

What high honor the Master has conferred on us in giving to all His followers the use of His Name at all times for all they desire — for this is what is involved in the verses we have been considering. The only limitation is on our side — that we ask only things consistent with His name and character.

Here again we are dependent on the help of the Holy Spirit to know how to use the name of Jesus aright. Instructing His disciples in the art of prayer, He said, "Until now you have asked for nothing in My name. . . . *In that day* you will ask in My name" (John 16:24, 26; italics added). In what day? The day when the Holy Spirit would be outpoured and begin His full ministry in their lives, teaching them "all the truth" (John 16:13).

He would interpret to them the petitions that were consistent with the name of Christ and were therefore assured of answer.

Before He returned to heaven, Jesus committed His interests into the hands of failing and frail men. He signed a power of attorney in their favor entitling them — and us — to use His name in drawing on the bank of heaven for any needful supplies for the welfare of His work.

PRAYER

Eternal Father, who didst give Thine only Son the Name most dear to Thee and needful for mankind, betokening not His majesty but our salvation: we pray Thee to set the Name of Jesus high above every name, and to plant in every heart the love of the only Saviour, who liveth and reigneth with Thee and the Holy Spirit, one God, world without end.

CAMBRIDGE BEDE BOOK

QUESTIONS

1. Praying in the Name of Jesus is to pray in union with the life and mind of Christ. What is involved in this statement?
2. Follow through the way the apostles used the powerful name of Jesus in Acts 2-4.

9

Praying in the Spirit

The Spirit Himself intercedes for us (Rom 8:26).

In the previous lessons in the school of prayer we analyzed the various elements in prayer, reviewed the prayer life of the Master Teacher, showed the place the promises of God play in prayer, and considered two of the conditions of answered prayer. We now come to the extremely important lesson of the part played by the Holy Spirit in the prayer life of the disciple of Christ.

"True prayer," wrote Samuel M. Zwemer, "is God the Holy Spirit talking to God the Father in the name of God the Son, and the believer's heart is the prayer-room."[1]

There is scriptural warrant for asserting that our chronic disinclination and reluctance to pray, as well as our ignorance of how to pray aright, find their complete answer in the ministry of the Holy Spirit in our hearts. Hence Paul's injunction, "Pray at all times in the Spirit" (Eph 6:18).

The Holy Spirit is the Source and Sustainer of our spiritual life. "If we live by the Spirit, let us also walk by the Spirit" (Gal 5:25). Since prayer is represented in Scripture as an essential factor in progress in the Christian life, it is not surprising to find that the Spirit of God is deeply involved in this sphere.

THE SPIRIT AND THE WORD

It hardly need be said that to pray in the Spirit means to pray in harmony with *the Word of God*, which He has inspired. He does not speak with two voices. He will never move us to pray for something that is not sanctioned by Scripture.

"There is an inseparable union between the Spirit, the Word and prayer," writes H. W. Frost, "which indicates that the Spirit will always lead the saint to make much of the Word, and especially God's promises in the Word. . . . This explains the fact that the great pray-ers have always been great students of the Word."[2]

It naturally follows that praying in the Spirit means to pray in harmony with *the will of God*. Being God Himself, the Spirit knows and can interpret God's will to us. Indeed, this is one of the very reasons why He has been given to the Church. "He intercedes for the saints according to the will of God" (Rom 8:27). We can therefore count on Him to enable us to pray in harmony with the will of God.

Prayer in the Spirit is prayer whose supreme object is *the glory of God*, and only in a secondary sense is it a blessing for ourselves or for others. This is not natural to us, for it is our natural tendency to be more concerned with our own interests and glory. The Holy Spirit will help us in this weakness, and will impart the motivation to shift our center from self to God.

Samuel Chadwick points out that the Holy Spirit never works alone — it is always in cooperation with men. "He depends upon human cooperation for the mediation of His mind, the manifestation of His truth, and the effectual working of His will. . . . We pray in the Spirit, and the Spirit maketh intercession for us."[3]

OUR TWO ADVOCATES

In this prayer life, the believer has the aid of two Advocates who continually make themselves available and plead his cause. How rich we are through this twofold ministry.

The Son of God intercedes for us before the throne of glory, securing for us the benefits of His mediatorial work. "If anyone sins, we have an Advocate with the Father, Jesus Christ the righteous" (1 John 2:1). We are thus the objects of His advocacy and intercession, which He carries on apart from us in heaven.

The Spirit of God is Christ's Advocate in our hearts to meet our deepest needs. In announcing the advent of the Holy Spirit, Jesus said, "If I do not go away, the Helper [Advocate, or Intercessor] shall not come to you; but if I go, I will send Him to you" (John 16:7). "You know Him because He abides with you, and will be in you" (John 14:17). Paul gives further light on His activity in prayer. "The Spirit Himself intercedes for us with groanings too deep for words" (Rom 8:26). We are thus the vehicles of the Spirit's intercession, which He carries on within us, through our redeemed personalities.

Writing on this aspect of the Spirit's ministry, Andrew Murray said,

> Just as wonderful and real is the divine work of God on the throne graciously hearing, and by His mighty power answering prayer. Just as divine as is the work of the Son, interceding and securing and transmitting the answer from above, is the work of the Holy Spirit in us in the prayer that awaits and obtains the answer. The intercession *within* is as divine as the intercession above.[4]

Weakness and inadequacy in the art of prayer are not surprising to God. He never intended that prayer should

be left to our own unaided faculties. So He gave the Holy
Spirit to instruct, inspire, and illumine our hearts and
minds. Unaided by Him, we would be likely to pray for
things not only contrary to God's will but injurious to
ourselves.

WHAT DOES IT MEAN TO
PRAY "IN THE SPIRIT"?

We must first understand the meaning of the phrase,
"in the Spirit." The text (Eph 6:18) is literally, "in
spirit," without the definite article. H. C. G. Moule interprets it as meaning surrounded by His presence and
power. "The Holy Spirit was to be 'the Place' of the
prayer, in the sense of being the surrounding, penetrating, transforming atmosphere of the spirit of the praying
Christian."[5]

Kenneth Wuest points out that "in the Spirit" is
locative of sphere. That is, all true prayer is exercised in
the sphere of the Holy Spirit, motivated and empowered
by Him. The expression *praying in the Holy Spirit* is
also instrumental of means. We pray by means of the
Holy Spirit, in dependence on Him.[6]

It is clear that praying in the Spirit means much more
than praying by the Spirit's help, although that is included. We pray by means of and in dependence on the
Spirit's help, but the Spirit is the atmosphere in which
the believer lives. So long as He is ungrieved, He is able
to guide us in our petitions and create in us the faith that
claims the answer. Our prayers will then be in substance
the same as the intercessions of the Spirit within.

So, praying in the Spirit is praying along the same
lines, about the same things, and in the same Name as
the Holy Spirit.

HOW DOES THE SPIRIT HELP
US IN PRAYER?

1. It is He who introduces us into the presence of the Father. "For through Him we . . . have our access in one Spirit to the Father" (Eph 2:18). The picture behind *access* is that of a court official who introduces people who desire an audience with the king. This is exactly what the Spirit does for us.

2. As "the Spirit of grace and of supplication" (Zech 12:10), He overcomes our reluctance, working in us the desire to pray. He graciously yet faithfully reveals to us our true heart-needs, and He leads us to seek their fulfillment in prayer.

3. He imparts a sense of sonship and acceptance that creates freedom and confidence in the presence of God. "God has sent forth the Spirit of His Son into our hearts, crying, 'Abba! Father!'" (Gal 4:6). Children are uninhibited in the presence of an understanding and loving father, and so may we be in our prayers.

4. He helps us in the ignorance of our minds and in the infirmities of our bodies, as well as in the maladies of the soul. "In the same way the Spirit helps our weaknesses; for we do not know how to pray as we should" (Rom 8:26), or as it is in the King James Version, "We know not what we should pray for as we ought."

We can count on the Spirit's aid in guiding us into the will of God through illumining Scripture to us and through stimulating and directing our mental processes. He also purifies our desires and redirects them towards the will of God, for He alone knows and can interpret God's will and purpose. "The thoughts of God no one knows except the Spirit of God" (1 Cor 2:11). He also helps by improving our motivation and inspiring confidence and faith in a loving Father.

5. He takes our faltering and imperfect prayers, adds to them the incense of the merits of Christ, and puts them in a form acceptable to our heavenly Father. "Another angel came and stood at the altar, holding a golden censer; and much incense was given to him, that he might add it to the prayers of all the saints upon the golden altar which was before the throne" (Rev 8:3). He takes our inarticulate groanings and infuses the right meaning into them.

6. He lays special burdens of prayer on the believer who is sensitively walking in fellowship with Him. Such a burden, intolerable at times, was laid on the prophets; often they could get relief only through prolonged and earnest prayer.

Daniel 10:2-3 refers to one such experience: "In those days I, Daniel, had been mourning for three entire weeks. I did not eat any tasty food, nor did meat or wine enter my mouth, nor did I use any ointment at all, until the entire three weeks were completed." But the answer came at the proper time — God's time.

When He lays such prayer-burdens on the hearts of His children, He intends to answer the prayer through their intercessions. He will impart the strength to pray through until the answer comes.

The foregoing considerations would lead us to conclude that to be able to pray prevailingly, we must be filled with the Holy Spirit. "We are never really men of prayer in the best sense, until we are filled with the Holy Spirit."

This necessity is emphasized by J. Stuart Holden:

> Here is the secret of prevailing prayer, to pray under a direct inspiration of the Holy Spirit, whose petitions for

us and through us are always according to the Divine
purpose, and hence certain of answer. "Praying in the
Holy Ghost is but co-operating with the will of God, and
such prayer is always victorious. How many Christians
there are who cannot pray, and who seek by effort, resolve, joining prayer circles, etc., to cultivate in themselves the "holy art of intercession," and all to no purpose. Here for them and for all is the only secret of a real
prayer life — "Be filled with the Spirit," who is "the
Spirit of grace and supplication."[7]

The prayers I make will then be sweet indeed
If Thou the Spirit give by which I pray:
My unassisted heart is barren clay,
That of its nature self can nothing feed;
Of good and pious works Thou art the seed,
That quickens only when Thou say'st it may;
Unless Thou show to us Thine own true way
No man can find it: Father! Thou must lead.

MICHELANGELO

PRAYER

O Holy Spirit, Giver of light and life, impart to us
thoughts higher than our own thoughts, and prayers
better than our own prayers, and powers beyond our
own powers; that we may spend and be spent in the
ways of love and goodness, after the perfect image of our
Lord and Saviour, Jesus Christ.

ANONYMOUS

QUESTIONS

1. What does Romans 8:26-27 teach about the part played by
God the Father and God the Spirit in the prayer life of the
believer?
2. In what way does being filled with the Spirit improve the
quality of one's prayer life?

10

The Prayer of Faith

Have faith in God (Mark 11:22).

We come now to a spiritual principle of overriding importance in relation to answered prayer. It is enunciated in Hebrews 11:6: "And without faith it is *impossible* to please Him, for he who comes to God *must believe* that He is, and that He is a rewarder of those who seek Him" (italics added). There is no acceptable substitute for faith. Faith feeds on the pledged Word of God, and flourishes in the atmosphere of His presence.

It has been said that just as there are two pairs of eyes, natural and spiritual eyes, so there are two kinds of faith, natural and spiritual faith. Natural faith is common to us all and is the basis of community life. We post a letter in the faith that the postal authorities will deliver it to the addressee, and our faith is usually rewarded. Business runs on the basis of natural faith.

Both natural and spiritual faith must have a sufficient basis. If I had no faith in the postal system, I would not pay out the money to post a letter. Behind business transactions, the faith of the businessman rests on the moral integrity and financial resources of his client.

But spiritual faith is the possession only of Christians. It views things through spiritual eyes and perceives

things invisible to the natural eye. Faith is the substance
of, the substantiating of, the giving substance to, things
not seen (Heb 11:1). Such faith is not inherent in human
nature, but is a gift of God's grace (Eph 2:8).

THE BASIS OF THE PRAYER OF FAITH

What, then, constitutes an adequate basis for the
prayer of faith?

On the negative side, it is not the evidence of outward
circumstances. The prayer of faith often finds its grand-
est opportunity in the utterly impossible situation, in
the absence of any tangible encouragement to believe.
Elijah's prayer of faith for rain triumphed in spite of the
six-times-repeated report from his servant that the sky
remained cloudless (1 Kings 18:41-45). Faith does not
require external confirmation, but believes God in spite
of appearances.

Nor does faith require or demand a sign to shore it up.
Christians sometimes speak of putting out a fleece as
Gideon did to determine what is the will of God. But was
not God's response to Gideon's twice-repeated request a
gracious concession to the feebleness of his faith rather
than a reward for its strength (Judges 6:36-40)? Jesus
constantly deprecated the seeking of a sign.

Thomas refused to be satisfied that the Lord had really
risen from the dead apart from the evidence of his own
senses. To him Jesus gave the gentle yet encouraging
rebuke: "Because you have seen Me, have you believed?
Blessed are they who did not see, and yet believed"
(John 20:29).

Nor do our feelings and emotional reactions constitute an adequate basis for the prayer of faith. When we
instruct someone seeking salvation, we are careful to
point out that he is assured of his salvation not because

he feels saved, but because he reposes his faith in the Saviour; and faith is independent of feelings. Feelings are no more a basis of faith for the believer than for the unbeliever. Faith trusts God in spite of the absence or contradiction of feelings.

On the positive side, the prayer of faith finds its warrant in the promises of the Word of God, applied to our hearts by the Spirit of God. It is a divinely given intuition and assurance that God has answered our prayer and granted our request. It is not the outcome of trying to believe, but is effortless confidence in God. When a man and his wife are deeply in love, it is no effort for them to trust each other.

HOW CAN WE BE SURE?

But how are we to distinguish between mere natural desires and the promptings of the Holy Spirit? John comes to our assistance on this point: "And this is the confidence which we have before Him, that, if we ask anything according to His will, He hears us. And if we know that He hears us in whatever we ask, *we know that we have the requests which we have asked from Him*" (1 John 5:14-15, italics added). This is one of the key verses relating to our subject.

We must first satisfy ourselves that our request is in harmony with the will of God, as previously suggested. Once we are sure of this, we know that He hears us, because we believe Him to be true to His pledged word. That being so, John says we know that we have — not will have, but have obtained — our request. The actual enjoyment of the prayed-for blessing may be in the future, but faith regards it as already in possession.

A man who lived in a New Zealand city had a son who, in spite of a godly upbringing, was quite unre-

sponsive to the Gospel message. The father had prayed
most earnestly for his son's salvation, but had seen no
change in his lifestyle or attitude to God. Suddenly the
son was killed in an accident. The father was naturally
distressed at the untimely death of his son, but with
quiet assurance he told sympathizing friends that he
was confident he and his son would meet in heaven —
and this in spite of any evidence to support his belief.

A few weeks later, a young man came to visit the
father. The young man had known the son.

"We will meet your son in heaven," he said.

"Yes, I am sure of that," replied the father. "God has
given me that assurance."

"Oh, I know more than that," was the reply. "A week
before he was killed, we attended an evangelistic service conducted by Herbert Booth, son of the founder of
the Salvation Army. When an invitation to accept Christ
was given, your son went forward, and I accompanied
him."

The reply of the father to this astonishing piece of
news was: "Of course I am delighted to hear what you
tell me, but I am no more sure now that we shall meet in
heaven than I was before you told me."[1]

Faith believes that it has received the answer, even in
the absence of any confirmatory evidence.

A STAGGERINGLY INCLUSIVE PROMISE

The parallel promise of Mark 11:24 seems so stagger-
ingly universal and inclusive in its implications that our
innate unbelief causes us to feel that it surely cannot
mean just what it says. "All things [what things soever,
KJV] for which you pray and ask, believe that you *have
received* them, and they shall be granted you" (italics
added). Our natural tendency is to tone the statement

down somewhat so as to bring it into the realm of the reasonable or probable. Can it really mean that if I want something, all I need to do is to pray and ask?

The answer is that "all things" and "what things soever" mean exactly what they say, but in the second clause there is a limitation implied — not on God's side, but on ours. For it is impossible for a believer to exercise faith for something that is beyond the scope of the will of God. If faith is the gift of God, and it is, He will not give it to someone in order to encourage him to do something contrary to His will.

The praying Christian will be able to believe all that is sanctioned by the Word of God and witnessed to by the Spirit. His faith will flow from his praying. It is in the atmosphere of prayer that the Holy Spirit nurtures and develops our faith, or on the other hand, indicates to us that what we desire is contrary to God's will.

In *Behind the Ranges*, James O. Fraser of Lisuland recounts his experience as he learned the possibilities and potency of the prayer of faith.

> "'The prayer of faith" [is] a definite request . . . made in definite faith for a definite answer. . . .
>
> In my own case here . . . I have definitely asked the Lord for several hundred families of Lisu believers. There are upwards of two thousand Lisu families in the district altogether. It might be said, "Why do you not ask for a thousand?" I answer quite frankly, because I have not faith for a thousand. . . .
>
> I prayed continually for the Tengyueh Lisu for over four years, asking many times that several hundreds of families might be turned to God. This was only general prayer, however. God was dealing with me in the meantime. . . . Then near the end of November . . . (1914), . . . this same petition came to me as a definite burden. . . .

I recognized the burden clearly. And it was an actual burden: it burdened me. I went to my room alone one afternoon and knelt in prayer. I knew that the time had come for the prayer of faith. And then, fully knowing what I was doing and what it might cost me, I definitely committed myself to this petition in faith. I "cast my burden upon the Lord." I rose from my knees with the deep, restful conviction that I had already received the answer.... And since then (nearly a year ago now) I have never had anything but peace and joy ... in holding to the ground already claimed and taken. I have never repeated the request and never will: there is no need.... The past can never be undone, never need be redone. It is a solemn thing to enter into a faith-covenant with God. It is binding on both parties. You lift up your hand to God; ... you definitely ask for and definitely receive His proffered gift; then do not go back on your faith, even if you live to be a hundred.[2]

When Fraser wrote the above, the answer was still in the future; but in God's time a glorious answer was given and thousands of Lisu turned to the Lord. Was his stand of faith contested? Hear his further testimony:

We often have to strive and wrestle in prayer ... before we attain this quiet, restful faith.... However, once we attain to a real faith, all the forces of hell are impotent to annul it. What then? They retire and muster their forces on this plot of ground which God has pledged Himself to give us, and contest every inch of it. The real battle begins when the prayer of faith has been offered. But, praise the Lord! we are on the winning side. Let us read and re-read the tenth chapter of Joshua, and never talk about defeat again.[3]

The victories won by prayer,
By prayer must still be held;

The foe retreats, but only when
By prayer he is compelled.

ANONYMOUS

It is worthy of note that in Elijah's prevailing prayer there were three important factors involved. (1) He based his prayer on a definite promise of God (1 Kings 18:1). (2) He fulfilled the condition attached to the promise (18:2). (3) He persevered in the prayer of faith in spite of the adverse report brought by sight (18:43). To his servant who brought the report, "he said, 'Go back' seven times." Note the progression. "There is nothing." "Behold, a cloud as small as a man's hand" (18:44). "There was a great rain" (18:45, KJV). James assures us that Elijah's prayer is a model prayer of faith (James 5:17-18).

Another classic example of the prayer of faith is recounted in *The Diary of George Mueller*. He writes:

> This is, perhaps, of all days the most remarkable so far as regards the funds. When I was in prayer this morning respecting them, *I was enabled firmly to believe* that the Lord would send help, though all seemed dark as to natural appearances. At twelve o'clock I met as usual with the brethren and sisters in prayer. There had come in only one shilling which, except twopence, had already been spent because of the great need. . . . Neither in the Infants' nor Boys' Orphan houses was there bread enough for tea, nor money to buy milk. Lower we had never been, perhaps never so low. We gave ourselves now unitedly to prayer, laying the case in simplicity before the Lord. . . . We continued for a while silently in prayer. . . . At last we rose from our knees. I said, "God will surely send help." The words had not quite passed my lips when I saw a letter lying on the table which had been brought while we were in prayer. It was from my

wife, containing another letter with £10 for the orphans. The prayer of faith had its reward.[4]

Isabel Kuhn tells how she and her husband were experiencing great opposition in a heathen village in South China. The people were deeply convicted, but could not break from their sinful customs. Then something happened.

"The last two days, without any explanation that we could discover, a sudden and astounding change took place," she wrote. Glorious victories were gained and quarrels settled. They did not know it, but a letter giving the explanation was already on the way. She had noted the date in her diary, and said to her husband, "I am sure someone in the homelands is specially praying for us." Two months passed, and then a letter.

"John, you read this while I get my diary." This is what he read:

> I must write and tell you what happened today. All morning I could not do my housework because of the burden on me concerning Three Clan Village. So finally I went to the telephone and called Mrs. W——. She said she had been feeling the same way and suggested we call Mrs. J——. and all go to prayer together. We did so, each in her own kitchen. We spent the morning in intercession for three quarrelling clans. We feel God has answered. You will know?

The date on the diary exactly corresponded with the victory gained in Three Clan Village.[5]

To conclude this study, let us recapitulate in the words of Hudson Taylor: "Faith is reliance on the trustworthiness of those with whom we transact business. Our faith is the recognition of God's faithfulness. It is so blessed to leave our faith out of account, and to be so occupied with God's faithfulness that we cannot raise any question whatsoever."[6]

PRAYER

Blessed Jesus, it is Thyself in whom our faith must be rooted if it is to grow strong. Thy work has freed us from the power of sin, and opened the way to the Father; Thy Spirit is always drawing us upwards into a life of perfect faith and confidence; we are assured that in Thy teaching we shall learn to pray the prayer of faith. Thou wilt train us to pray so that we believe that we receive, to believe that we really have what we ask. Lord, teach me so to love and trust Thee that my soul may have in Thee assurance that I am heard.

ANONYMOUS

QUESTIONS

1. If the Holy Spirit has been grieved in our lives, what effect would that have on our ability to pray the prayer of faith? What should we do?
2. How can our faith be increased so that we can confidently ask God for larger answers?

11

Shameless Persistence

Because of his importunity (Luke 11:8, KJV).

We come now to a requirement in prayer that is rather surprising, and to some, not a little puzzling. It seems that God is moved to answer our prayers in response to a persistence that will not take no for an answer — shameless persistence, someone rendered it.

Jesus employed varied methods of imparting truth to His disciples. Sometimes He employed paradox, sometimes parables. In some parables truth was taught by comparison, in others by contrast. He adopted the latter in enforcing the necessity of importunity and perseverance in prayer, and told two parables.

THE THREE FRIENDS (Luke 11:5-8)

There are three persons in this parable — the one spoken for, the one who speaks, and the one appealed to. The Lord vividly contrasts the reluctance and selfishness of the friend appealed to, with the openhanded and openhearted generosity of the heavenly Father. The man appealed to was not concerned about his friend's distress. The argument runs: If even a self-centered and ungenerous human being to whom sleep was more important than his friend's distress and need will reluctantly rise at midnight and supply the need because of

his friend's shameless persistence, how much more will
God be moved by persistent entreaty to meet His child's
need!

"Even though he will not get up and give him anything because he is his friend, yet because of his persistence he will get up and give him as much as he needs"
(v. 8).

THE UNPRINCIPLED JUDGE (Luke 18:1-8)

The parable of the heartless and unprincipled judge,
who had neither reverence for God nor respect for men,
teaches the same lesson even more strongly. If the de-
fenseless but troublesome widow by her shameless persistence overcame the reluctance of the unjust judge to
do her justice, how much more will the believer be
speedily vindicated in the court of heaven, where he has
a strong Advocate whose character is the exact opposite
of the judge's.

"Shall not God bring about justice for His elect, who
cry to Him day and night, and will He delay long over
them? I tell you that He will bring about justice for them
speedily" (vv. 7-8).

In both parables, Jesus is careful to vindicate the
character of God and to reveal His true nature and attitude. "If you then, being evil, know how to give good
gifts to your children, *how much more* shall your Father
who is in heaven give what is good to those who ask
Him!" (Matt 7:11, italics added). God is neither a selfish
neighbor nor a crooked judge dispensing reluctant justice to a wronged widow simply because his comfort
was being disturbed by her persistence.

The lesson is that lukewarmness in prayer, as in everything else, is nauseating to God, and comes away
empty-handed. On the other hand, shameless persis-

tence, the importunity that will not be denied, returns with the answer in its hands.

Do our prayers lack urgency? Can we do without the thing for which we are asking? Or is it something we must have at all costs? John Knox cried, "Give me Scotland or I die." The saint and patriot would not be denied.

Jesus encourages us to believe that this is the kind of praying that receives an answer. Importunity is an important element in answered prayer.

Adoniram Judson, the great missionary to Burma, was a man of prayer. "God loves importunate prayer so much," he said, "that He will not give us much blessing without it. And the reason He loves such prayer is that He loves us, and knows that it is a necessary preparation for our receiving the richest blessing He is waiting and longing to bestow.

"I never prayed sincerely and earnestly for anything but it came at some time — no matter at how distant a day, somehow, in some shape, probably the last I would have devised, it came."[1]

WHY IS IMPORTUNITY NECESSARY?

Since God is a loving heavenly Father who knows all our needs better than we do, why should He require us to importune Him? Why does He not just grant our requests, as He is well able to do?

This is somewhat of a mystery, and the answer does not appear on the surface. We can be assured that there is no reluctance on God's part to give us whatever is good for us. He does not need to be coaxed, for He is not capricious. Prayer is not a means of extorting blessing from unwilling fingers. The "how much more" of Matthew 7:11 affirms this with emphasis. The answer must be sought elsewhere. The necessity must lie in us, not in God. It is not God who is under test, but our own spiritual maturity.

Dr. W. E. Biederwolf makes the interesting suggestion that importunity is one of the instructors in God's training school for Christian culture. God does not always grant the answer to prayer at once because the petitioner is not yet in a fit state to receive what he asks. There is something God desires to do in him before He answers the prayer.

There may be some lack of yieldedness, or some failure to master some previous spiritual lesson. So while He does not deny the request, He withholds the answer until, through persevering prayer, the end He has in view is achieved.

May this not be in part the explanation of some of God's seeming delays? His delays are always delays of love, not of caprice. "Men would pluck their mercies green; God would have them ripe."

AN ATHLETIC OF THE SOUL

Canon W. Hay Aitken refers to prayer as "an athletic of the soul" that is designed to render our desires more intense by giving them adequate expression, to exercise the will in its highest functions, and to bring us into closer touch with God. It will also test the reality and sincerity of our faith, and save it from being superficial. Importunity rouses the slumbering capacities of the soul and prepares the way for faith.[2]

There may be other reasons why the divine response tarries and importunity is needed. Here are some suggestions.

1. We may be asking without greatly caring about the

issue. If we are not in earnest, why should God bestir Himself? We shall find Him when we seek with all our hearts.

2. We may be asking for selfish reasons, and the discipline of delay is necessary to purge us of this. Selfish motivation is self-defeating in prayer.

3. We may unconsciously be unwilling to pay the price involved in the answering of our prayers, and our Father desires us to face up to this fact.

4. We may be misinterpreting what God is doing in our lives in answer to our prayers. This was the case with John Newton, the converted slave-trader. He gives his testimony in verse:

> I asked the Lord, that I may grow
> In faith, and love, and every grace;
> Might more of his salvation know,
> And seek more earnestly his face.
> . . . .
> I hoped that in some favoured hour,
> At once he'd answer my request;
> And by his love's constraining power,
> Subdue my sins, and give me rest.
>
> Instead of this, he made me feel
> The hidden evils of my heart;
> And let the angry powers of hell
> Assault my soul in every part.
>
> Yea more, with his own hand he seemed
> Intent to aggravate my woe;
> Crossed all the fair designs I schemed,
> Blasted my gourds, and laid me low.
>
> Lord, why is this, I trembling cried,
> Wilt thou pursue thy worm to death?
> " 'Tis in this way," the Lord replied,
> "I answer prayer for grace and faith.

"These inward trials I employ,
From self and pride to set thee free;
And break thy schemes of earthly joy,
That thou mayst seek thy all in me."

God's dual method with His servant was to reveal to
him the inherent evil of his heart so that he would be
motivated to claim importunately from God the
blessing he was then fitted to receive.
5. Another possible reason for God's apparent delay or
denial of an answer is put forward to Dr. D. M. McIn-
tyre: it secures our humble dependence on God.[3] If
He bestowed our desires as gifts of nature and did not
want our solicitations, we would tend to become
independent of Him. "Otherwise, you may say in
your heart, 'My power and the strength of my hand
made me this wealth,'" was God's warning to His
people. "You shall remember the LORD your God, for
it is He who is giving you power to make wealth"
(Deut 8:17-18).

OUR PART NOT YET FULLY DONE

For our encouragement, we should remember that the
walls of Jericho did not fall until the Israelites had circled them a full thirteen times and then shouted the
shout of faith (Josh 6:1-20). We may have circled our
prayer-Jericho the full thirteen times, and yet the answer
has not come. Why? Could it be that God is waiting to
hear the shout of faith? Perhaps that is the reason the
forbidding walls are still intact. He delights to see us
step out in faith upon His naked promise.

Unanswered yet? Nay, do not say unanswered,
   Perhaps your part is not yet wholly done,

The work began when first your prayer was uttered,
  And God will finish what He has begun.
Keep incense burning at the shrine of prayer,
  And glory shall descend sometime, somewhere.
Unanswered yet? Faith cannot be unanswered;
  Her feet are firmly planted on the Rock;
Amid the wildest storms she stands undaunted,
  Nor quails before the loudest thunder shock.
She knows Omnipotence has heard her prayer,
  And cries, "It shall be done sometime, somewhere."

OPHELIA GUYON BROWNING

TWO IMPORTUNATE INTERCESSORS

Abraham and Elijah stand in contrast in two prayer engagements.

In his intercession for Sodom, Abraham almost prevailed, but failed to receive the complete answer because of failure in importunity (Gen 18:16-33). Elijah, on the other hand, in his prayer for rain on Mount Carmel, experienced an overflowing answer (1 Kings 18:42-45). The reason is instructive.

Abraham was an intimate friend of God. In one of his conversations with God, God revealed to him the impending judgment on Sodom. He interceded for his nephew Lot and the people of Sodom in a prayer of mixed argument, audacity, and humility.

It was a most remarkable prayer. Time and again Abraham enlarged his demand—fifty righteous, forty-five, forty, thirty, twenty, ten—and then he stopped praying. There was no reason to suppose God's mercy was exhausted. But while Abraham received a partial answer and Lot was delivered, Sodom was destroyed. His intercession was unsuccessful because of failure in importunity.

Elijah pressed his suit on behalf of his drought-stricken nation, and refused to take no for an answer. Seven times, strong in faith, he pled with God, and the full answer came.

Is it without significance that Elijah prayed seven times—the number of perfection and fullness—while Abraham stopped at six times, the number of human frailty? Abraham stopped asking before God stopped answering. Let us become "seven-times prayers."

> Faith, mighty faith the promise sees,
> And looks to God alone;
> Laughs at impossibilities,
> And cries, It shall be done!
>
> C. WESLEY

PRAYER

Eternal God, who tarriest oft beyond the time we hope for, but not beyond the time appointed by Thee; from which cometh from Thee the truth that cannot lie, the counsel that cannot fail. Make us faithful to stand upon our watchtower, and to wait for what Thou wilt say to us; that by our faith we may live, and at the last behold Thy righteousness prevail; to the glory of Thy name.

ANONYMOUS

QUESTIONS

1. How can the idea of importunity be reconciled with submission to the will of God?
2. Can you think of other reasons God requires us to be importunate in prayer?

12

Post-Mortem on Unanswered Prayer

Because you ask with wrong motives (James 4:3).

Having considered some of the most important conditions of answered prayer, we come face to face with the fact that too many of our prayers go unanswered. This is a melancholy admission in view of the multiplicity of the promises God has made to the praying soul.

When a prudent businessman discovers that his business is running at a loss, he takes stock, draws up a balance sheet, discovers why he has made no profit, and takes remedial steps. Shall we be less prudent in our spiritual accounting? Have we ever sat down and honestly faced this question? Do we just accept the failure of some of our prayers fatalistically? Do we piously say, "Perhaps it was not God's will after all?" Or do we ask honest questions:

Am I sure my request was in harmony with God's will?

Did I really pray making use of Jesus' name?

Did I pray the prayer of faith and really expect the answer?

Was I praying from selfish motives?

Have I been importunate?

87

Did I depend on the Holy Spirit in my praying?

I am certain that God is more honored when we honestly face and confess our failures in prayer than when we piously ignore them. So let us conduct a postmortem, search out the causes, and remedy them. When we do this sincerely, we will experience an upgrading in the quality of our prayer life. Behind every unanswered prayer there is a reason, which we must discover for ourselves.

The apostle James asserts that the basic reason for every unanswered prayer is that in some way we have asked wrongly. "You ask and do not receive, because you ask with wrong motives" (James 4:3). There are other reasons for nonanswered prayer as well, and it is now our objective to examine these potential causes of failure.

POSSIBLE REASONS FOR FAILURE IN PRAYER

Here are some possible explanations for failure in prayer.

1. *Perhaps our faith has been resting on a wrong basis.* Could it be that we have been unconsciously substituting faith in *prayer* for faith in *God*? Have we been expecting our prayer to give the answer? Think this through carefully. We are nowhere in Scripture exhorted to put our faith in prayer, but we are commanded, "Have faith in God" (Mark 11:22). If our faith is directed toward and reposes in the God to whom we pray, our faith will not stumble even if He does not exactly do what we may ask. In spite of the popular motto, it is not prayer that changes things, but God who changes things when we conform to His laws for answered prayer.

Or could it be that we have been unconsciously substituting faith in our *faith* for faith in God? This may sound trite, but it is a very real possibility. When we say, "My faith is so small; I can't believe that God will do it," are we not admitting that we are depending on the quantity of our faith rather than resting on the faithful God for the answer?

It is true that "without faith it is impossible to please Him (Heb 11:6), but faith is like eyesight. Like eyesight, faith does not exist apart from the object on which it is focused. Have you ever seen eyesight? There is no such thing as faith in the abstract. I am to focus my faith on God, and not to have faith in my faith.

Or could it be that I have been relying on my earnestness and importunity in prayer to bring the answer, instead of relying on God Himself?

2. *There may be in our hearts a secret sympathy with sin.* If this is the case, our prayers will be effectually short-circuited, and our prayer life sabotaged.

In this connection, no statement could be more explicit than Psalm 66:18: "If I regard wickedness in my heart, the Lord will not hear." It is important to notice that the word "regard" does not merely mean to "look on," but to "hold on to, cling to."

The psalmist was enunciating a clear spiritual principle here. He claimed that he was not holding on to sin in his heart, and so could testify, "But certainly God has heard; He has given heed to the voice of my prayer" (Psalm 66:19). If we are to expect an answer to our prayers, we must make a clean break with sin.

3. *Perhaps the motive behind our prayers is not pure.* "You ask and do not receive, because you ask with wrong motives, so that you may spend it on your pleasures" (James 4:3).

God nowhere binds Himself to answer self-centered or selfish prayers. While He promises to meet all our genuine needs, He does not undertake to gratify all our selfish desires. In prayer for temporal things, we should carefully examine our motivation and ask, "Is this petition for God's glory, for my good, and for the good of others, or is it merely to gratify my own selfish desires?"

4. *Instead of having confidence in approaching God, we may be being held back by a condemning heart.* John the apostle assured those to whom he was writing that whatever condemns us in our conscience hinders prayer. Until known sin is judged and renounced, we pray and plead in vain. "Beloved, if our heart does not condemn us, we have confidence before God; and whatever we ask we receive from Him" (1 John 3:21-22).

If we know of some reason our conscience condemns us, it is for us to deal with it and do all in our power to put it right with God and man. Until we do, we will endeavor in vain to pray the prayer of faith. More often than not this is why we are unable to exercise appropriating faith when we pray.

What are we to do if some subtle sense of guilt and condemnation descends on our spirits? We examine our hearts, but can assign no reason for the distress. It is a nameless and ill-defined depression of spirit, a vague malaise that prevents the soul from rising to God in the prayer of faith. How is this condition to be met?

First, let us sincerely ask God to reveal to us if there is some real but unrecognized sin that lies at the root of this sense of condemnation. If He reveals something to us, let us put it right at the first opportunity. Confidence toward God will thus be restored, and our prayers will receive their answers.

But should there be no such revelation of sin, we are

justified in concluding that the obscuring cloud origi-
nates in enemy territory. Many have found it helpful to
pray in such circumstances, "Lord, if this sense of condemnation comes from Your Spirit's conviction, make
my sin clear to me and I shall confess and put it right.
But if it comes from Satan, then on the grounds of
Calvary's victory, I refuse and reject it."

This attitude of acceptance of the divine dealing but
rejection of the satanic intrusion has often brought deliverance and renewed freedom in prayer, for it is true
that "if our heart does not condemn us, we have confidence before God."

5. *We may be entertaining a bitter or unforgiving
spirit.* Jesus handled this possibility very faithfully. "I
say to you, all things for which you pray and ask, believe
that you have received them, and they shall be granted
you. And *whenever you stand praying, forgive,* if you
have anything against anyone; so that your Father also
who is in heaven may forgive you your transgressions"
(Mark 11:24-25, italics added).

These sobering words should convince us of the folly
of expecting an answer to our prayers when we are
cherishing unforgiving spirits. Because I have been forgiven, I must forgive. If I fail to do so, I will be unable to
pray with assurance of an answer.

Dr. H. A. Ironside told of a man who gave this testimony:

> For years I prayed for the conversion of an erring son,
> but all the time he seemed to go from bad to worse.
> During those years I had a bitter feeling in my heart
> towards a brother who, I felt, had grievously wronged
> me. I insisted upon reparation which he refused to make.
> Feeling my cause was just, I held this against him, and
> would not overlook it.

At last I realized that this was hindering prayer, I judged it before God and freely forgave. O the liberty as I then turned to God about my son! Soon I heard with joy of his conversion. Though far from home, he was brought under the power of the gospel and led to Christ. An unforgiving spirit explains why thousands of petitions go apparently unheeded.[1]

6. *Perhaps all is not right in the marital relationship.* This possibility is plainly envisaged in 1 Peter 3:1-7, a passage that treats the relationship that should exist between husband and wife, and the duties they owe to one another. The paragraph begins, "You wives, be submissive to your own husbands," and concludes, "You husbands likewise, live with your wives in an understanding way, as with a weaker vessel, since she is a woman; and grant her honor as a fellow-heir of the grace of life, *so that your prayers may not be hindered*" (italics added).

When husband and wife are one in heart and purpose, mutually recognizing the place assigned to each in Scripture and practicing the law of love, prayer is easy and confident. But when there is a lack of that mutuality, when there is selfishness in the intimate things of the marriage relationship, the prayer life of the couple becomes the first casualty. There may be a form of prayer maintained, but joy and spontaneity will depart and answers will be few.

When a growing family has daily evidence of such a lack of harmony and sympathy between its parents, that need can prove in itself a tragic hindrance to the answer of parental prayers. On the other hand, when the family has daily evidence of mutual and sacrificial love, the way is open for the Spirit to work and answer the prayers of the parents.

7. *Our prayers are sometimes the outlet for unbelief and despair rather than the outpouring of faith.* A fundamental prayer-principle is given in Hebrews 11:6. Its absoluteness is impressive. "Without faith it is impossible to please Him, for he who comes to God must believe that He is, and that He is a rewarder of those who seek Him."

It is true that God invites us to pour out our hearts before Him and to unload our burdens at His feet. But we are to come to Him in the confidence of faith, not in the numbness of despair. Our God loves to be trusted. "Let him ask in faith without any doubting," exhorts James, "for the one who doubts is like the surf of the sea driven and tossed by the wind. For let not that man expect that he will receive anything from the Lord" (James 1:6-7).

One characteristic of a wave is that it never stays in the same place for two seconds. So it is with the unstable, double-souled, unbelieving man, says James (v. 8). Such a man puts his burden or problem in God's hands one minute and takes it back again the next, only to repeat the futile process. He believes one minute and doubts the next.

The psalmist, confident in the trustworthiness of his God, has a satisfying prescription for such a person: "Commit [and leave committed] your way to the LORD, trust also [and keep on trusting] in Him, and He will do it. . . . Rest in the LORD and wait patiently for Him" (Psalm 37:5, 7).

8. *Perhaps satanic resistance preventing the answer to our prayers from reaching us must be dealt with.* This was the experience of the prophet Daniel as he recorded it in Daniel 10:12-13:

> Then He said to me, 'Do not be afraid, Daniel, for from the first day that you set your heart on understanding

this and on humbling yourself before your God, your words were heard, and I have come in response to your words. But the prince of the kingdom of Persia was withstanding me for twenty-one days; then behold, Michael, one of the chief princes, came to help me, for I had been left there with the kings of Persia.

The messenger whom God had dispatched in answer to Daniel's prayer was detained on the way for three weeks, and it was only through the help of Michael, the archangel, that there had been a successful completion of his mission.

We should recognize that unseen forces rule the world. In this instance there was conflict between the spiritual forces behind the kings of Persia and the messengers from God. This is an area of truth of which we know little, but it does throw light on the mystery of unanswered prayer.

The answer to Daniel's prayer began in the heavenly sphere before it was evident on earth (v. 12). Satan, as always, opposed the purpose of God, but he did not succeed. Daniel was mystified by God's delay in answering his prayers, and it was only after he had persevered in prayer that he learned the real reason. It was not that his prayers had not been heard, but that they had triggered a conflict in the heavenly realm. That conflict was brought to a successful conclusion only by the intervention of God. We little know what supernatural forces are unleashed when we pray the prayer of faith.

> Ah dearest Lord! I cannot pray,
>   My fancy is not free;
> Unmannerly distractions come,
>   And force my thoughts from Thee.

. . . .

My very flesh has restless fits;
  My changeful limbs conspire
With all these phantoms of the mind
  My inner self to tire.

I cannot pray; yet, Lord! Thou knowst
  The pain it is to me
To have my vainly struggling thoughts
  Thus torn away from Thee.

. . . .
Yet Thou art oft most present, Lord!
  In weak distracted prayer:
A sinner out of heart with self
  Most often finds Thee there.

. . . .
My Saviour! why should I complain
  And why fear aught but sin?
Distractions are but outward things;
  Thy peace dwells far within.

F. W. FABER

PRAYER

Blessed Lord, Thy words are faithful and true. It must be because I pray amiss that my experience of answered prayer is not clearer. It must be because I live too little in the Spirit that my prayer is too little in the Spirit, and that the power for the prayer of faith is wanting. Lord, teach me to pray! Lord Jesus, I trust Thee for it; teach me to pray in faith.

ANDREW MURRAY

QUESTIONS

1. God sometimes answers prayer by giving something other than what was prayed for. Is this a valid proposition?
2. How can we tell whether nonanswer of our prayer is a delay or a denial?

13

Moving Men Through God

Why could not we? (Matt 17:19, KJV).

In an earlier lesson intercession was defined, and now we shall consider the subject in greater detail.

It is not irreverent to recognize as a fact that there are perplexing problems involved in the ministry of intercession. All Christian workers, and especially those engaged in pastoral or missionary work, frequently find themselves in situations in which the minds and hearts of men must be moved if the objectives the Christians have in view are to be achieved. In other words, we are involved in the complex problems of personality.

We may be confronted with a crisis that threatens the disintegration of our work. Or we have to meet strong opposition in a work we believe is in God's will. Or we are unable to secure unanimity in our group on important matters requiring decision. Or we face an impossible situation to which there seems to be no solution that would not cause serious misunderstanding or hurt someone else.

MOVING MEN THROUGH GOD

In circumstances like these, what are we to do? Can we expect to move men through God by our prayers?

Men are difficult objects to move. Prayer for material things is much less complex and demanding than that which involves the intricacies of the human heart. But God has placed in our hands a key with three words that will open this complicated lock—*Ask! Seek! Knock!* (Matt 7:7-8).

These words are often treated as though they were synonyms, alternative words for the one prayer. But it would seem that they refer to progressive acts of prayer, each more intense and demanding than the last. They represent an ascending climax, stages of increasing persistence.

Someone has seen in it the picture of a needy and importunate man who first asks the aid of a friend in some public place. On being rebuffed, he seeks his friend out at his home and renews the plea with increasing urgency. When the door is shut in his face, he refuses to go away, but keeps on knocking and demanding help until he receives it.

This is of course a parable of contrast that enforces a primary lesson. God desires us to be earnest to the point of persistency, of refusal to be denied, and He assures that He will grant the answer to such praying: "It *shall* be given to you—you *shall* find—it *shall* be opened" (italics added). We are thus encouraged to bring our insoluble problems to Him and are assured of answers.

But it is just here that we come face to face with the problem of human free will. Scripture makes it clear that God has endowed man with the godlike quality of self-determination and free will. That this subject is mysterious and open to varying views is admitted, but it is the view of many evangelical Christians that man possesses the awesome power of saying no to God as well as yes.

INTERCESSION AND FREE WILL

This poses a very real problem in intercession. Will God violate the free will of one person in order to answer the prayers of another? If by our prayers we can affect the conduct of a fellow man, does that not involve trespassing on his free will? And yet if our prayers cannot so influence him, what is the point in praying?

In our search for a solution, we must bear in mind certain factors.

1. *Intercession is a divine ordinance,* and whatever the problems encountered, believers must render obedience. We are exhorted to make "entreaties and prayers, petitions and thanksgivings . . . on behalf of all men" (1 Tim 2:1).

2. *In all God's actions He is consistent with Himself.* He cannot deny or contradict Himself. If He has bound Himself by a promise to answer the prayer of faith, He will undoubtedly do so, but not in a manner that is contrary to His divine nature. He will fulfill all He has undertaken to do, but in a way that is consistent with His own nature and attributes. It is axiomatic that no word or action of God will contradict any other word or action.

It could be contended that whereas our supplications do not change God's mind, they often produce such a change in us as to make it right and consistent for God to grant a favorable answer to the supplicant.

God obviously finds no inconsistency or conflict between prayer and the exercise of free will. When He exhorts us to pray for earthly rulers, there is implicit in the command the assurance that our prayers will make a difference; that they can move these men and significantly influence the course of national and international events. Otherwise, why pray? Whether we find an intel-

lectually satisfying and final answer to this prayer problem or not, the fact that God has commanded it should
be sufficient to satisfy faith, and we are under obligation
to obey.

And when we have prayed the prayer of faith in ac-
cordance with Mark 11:24, we can be assured that we
have received all that God can consistently grant us. We
can rest assured that He will exercise His divine influence on the subject of our prayers to the fullest possible
extent, short of encroaching on his free will, so as to
enable him to come to Christ or otherwise conform to
His will. We can be sure that He will choose the best
time and employ the best method to make His influence
felt.

But what if the prayer is not answered, in spite of the
sincerity of our desires and the earnestness of our pleas?
Some light is thrown on the perplexity by the fact that
our Lord Himself had to face the same problem. He did
not see His heart's desire for men realized in every case.
There were those over whom He had to utter the lament
of unrequited love: "O Jerusalem, Jerusalem . . . , how
often I wanted to gather your children together, just as a
hen gathers her brood under her wings, and you would
not have it!" (Luke 13:34). And on another occasion He
had to mourn: "You are unwilling to come to Me, that
you may have life" (John 5:40).

No failure in prayer or lack of concern for the people
could be laid at His door, as it can all too often be laid at
ours. But in some cases, in spite of this His prayers were
frustrated. Yet He refused to exercise His divine power
in order to compel them to come to Him. This is what is
involved in the solemn responsibility of being man. We
can say no to God.

This did not discourage Jesus from praying. He recognized the solemn fact, as we must, that in the final analysis the human will can become so debased that it can thwart the loving desires of God's heart. In these circumstances He did what we must do. He prayed and trustingly left the issue in the hands of His Father.

INTERCESSION AND PREDESTINATION

Another question naturally arises as we face the problems involved in intercession. How can we reconcile intercessory prayer with the doctrine of predestination? The crux of the problem probably lies in our wrong or inadequate understanding of that doctrine. But the question is sometimes put, "If God has already predetermined all that is going to happen, how can our praying make any real difference? Would not a later arrangement of events involve God in inconsistency or contradiction?"

This is a knotty problem that has exercised the minds of praying men in all ages, and different men have arrived at different conclusions. The most one can hope to do is to offer a suggestion that may at least give a little help. Since God has commanded us to pray, prayer must form part of His overall purpose. Since He has pledged Himself to answer these prayers, is it not reasonable to assume that in His scheme of things He has made full allowance for all the implications of prayer? Could it not be that our prayers form part of His plan and purpose, and indeed by the very factor that would bring that purpose about? If the foreordination of God is a valid objection to intercession, could it not also be contended that it is a valid objection to every other form of human activity?

In prayer we deal directly with God, and with men

only in a secondary sense. The goal of prayer is the ear of God. It is not our prayer that moves men, but the God to whom we pray. Prayer influences men by moving God to influence them. If a scheming Jacob could be entrusted with power with God and men (Gen 32:28), may we not, despite our failures, be entrusted with a similar ministry?

When Ezra returned to Jerusalem, he faced a situation typical of that experienced so often by Christian workers. He found his people in a tragically backslidden condition. He could not preach to them. How could he influence them to dissolve forbidden partnerships, to divorce forbidden wives and husbands, and to put right a hundred other irregularities? He could influence God to influence them!

So he gave himself to prayer and the confession of sins to which he had not been party. He pled with fasting for God's mercy on His people. No placid and pallid praying this! Weeping, he prostrated himself before God.

Before long "a very large assembly, men, women, and children, gathered to him from Israel; for the people wept bitterly" (Ezra 10:1). Intense and prevailing prayer moved men through God and achieved its end.

PRAYER

May God the Father and the Eternal High Priest, Jesus Christ, build us up in faith and truth and chastity, and grant to us our portion among the saints with all those who believe on our Lord Jesus Christ. We pray for all saints; for kings and rulers; for our persecutors and for enemies of the Cross; and for ourselves we pray that our fruit may abound and we may be made perfect in Christ Jesus our Lord.

POLYCARP

QUESTIONS

1. How can God, in order to answer prayer, interfere with the fixed and unchangeable laws that reign in the universe?
2. How can the foreknowledge of God be an encouragement in prayer?

14

The Pattern Prayer

Pray, then, in this way (Matt 6:9).

The Lord's Prayer was the first specific lesson on prayer that Jesus taught His disciples. They had been listening in to their Master while He was praying, and the experience had kindled in their hearts a yearning to know the same intimacy with the Father that He enjoyed. He answered them by giving them a model, or pattern, for prayer which has become the most widely used of all religious formularies.

It has, however, suffered greatly at the hands of its friends. Some neglect it, some recite it thoughtlessly, some postpone its application to the distant future, and only a minority exhaust its full possibilities.

The Lord foresaw the possibility of its misuse, and in the verses immediately preceding the prayer (Matt 6:5, 7) He warned His disciples of two perils that would beset its use. (1) They were not to pray as the hypocrites did (v. 5), who reserved their praying for public occasions. (2) They were not to pray as the heathen did (v. 7), merely heaping up empty and meaningless phrases.

The failure to heed this counsel has done more to rob this matchless prayer of its deep significance and blessing than anything else. It is reserved by most only for public recitation, and even then it tends to degenerate into the repetition of familiar words with little thought of their meaning.

While not ruling out its validity as a form of prayer to recite in public services, it is open to question whether this was our Lord's main objective in giving it. Indeed, the context is, "Go into your inner room, and . . . shut your door" (v. 6). It would appear that it is meant primarily, though not necessarily solely, for private use. Do we use it in private prayer?

In this prayer Jesus laid down the principles governing man's relationship to God, and these are relevant to believers in every age. It should be noted that He did not say, "Pray in these precise words," but, "Pray, then, in this way" (v. 9). He was giving a pattern, not an inflexible form. The exact words employed may vary greatly, while the individual prayer itself conforms to the pattern given.

DISTINCTIVE CHARACTERISTICS

Several things emerge as we study the prayer in detail (Matt 6:9-13).

1. *It defines the spirit in which we should pray.* It is to be in (a) an unselfish spirit—not "my" but "our"; (b) a filial spirit—"Father"; (c) a reverent spirit—"hallowed be Thy name"; (d) a loyal spirit—"Thy kingdom come"; (e) a submissive spirit—"Thy will be done"; (f) a dependent spirit—"Give us this day our daily bread"; (g) a penitent spirit—"Forgive us our debts"; and (h) a humble spirit—"Do not lead us into temptation." The spirit in which we pray is much more important than the words in which our prayers are clothed.

2. *It is brief yet profound.* Only fifty-five words, yet what breadth of application and depth of meaning. It

reaches the Greek rhetorical ideal of an ocean of truth in a drop of speech. There is no holy loquacity here, only six pointed petitions. Only God could compress so much meaning into so few words.

3. *It is wonderfully comprehensive.* It contrives to embody in embryo every desire of the praying heart. It combines every divine promise and every human aspiration. It summarizes all we should pray for. Nothing promised to the Christian is outside its scope.

4. *It is of universal application.* It covers all the needs common to humanity. It bears no mark of race or creed. People of every class and color have made it the expression of their hearts. It is the one religious formulary that is easily translatable into all languages.

5. *It reveals the priorities to be observed in prayer.* It is striking that the prayer is halfway through before the needs and desires of the petitioner are mentioned. This is the divine order, but not always the human practice. The heavenly is to have priority over the earthly.

6. *God is bound to answer every prayer that conforms to this pattern.* Can our prayer be brought within the scope of this prayer? Then it is certain of answer, for the pattern is divinely given.

THE PRAYER ITSELF

Now let us consider the prayer in some detail.

The invocation. "Our Father who art in heaven." In the place of prayer, selfishness is excluded. This is a prayer for the family of which God is the Father and we are members. God is the Father only of those who have entered His family by way of the new birth.

"Who art in heaven," someone has quaintly said, is not God's postal address. It indicates not so much His location as His elevation above man, His complete sep-

aration from man's corruption. "Our Father" awakens
love in our hearts; "Who art in heaven" engenders awe.
And these together constitute worship. The invocation
is a blending of intimacy and majesty.

Then follow three petitions concerning God and His
glory (vv. 9-10).

A concern for His name. "Hallowed be Thy name."
God's name is His nature, Himself, His personality as
revealed in Christ. To hallow anything is to treat it as
holy, to hold it in reverence. This petition asks that He
Himself will be universally and perpetually held in
reverence among men. He is to be given the unique
place His name demands. "A Christlike character is the
best way of hallowing the name of God."

This petition has missionary overtones. How can His
name be hallowed by people who have never heard it? A
true hallowing of His name will result in a passion to
make that name known.

A concern for His Kingdom. "Thy kingdom come." In
Jewish thought, the Kingdom means the reign, the
sovereignty of God. Why do not all men hallow God's
name? Because they belong to a rival kingdom presided
over by the prince of this world. They must first be
brought into the Kingdom before they will reverence the
King. This, too, has missionary implications.

The loyal disciple has a passion for the spread of His
Lord's sovereignty over the hearts of men here and now,
but he also longs to see the rejected Christ enthroned
and worshiped by all, and to this end he will pray.

Actually, the tense of the verb "come" points to a
climactic, not gradual, coming of His Kingdom. So it is
really a prayer for the second advent of Christ, this time
as enthroned King.

O the joy to see Thee reigning,
Thee my own beloved Lord;
Every tongue Thy name confessing,
Worship, honour, glory, blessing,
Brought to Thee with one accord.

FRANCES RIDLEY HAVERGAL

A concern for His will, and the fulfillment of His purposes on earth. This logically follows the preceding petition. The loyal believer will cherish a deep desire for the achieving of the purposes of God. He does not regard prayer merely as a means of getting his own will done, but as a means of ensuring that God's will is done in his own life and in that of others.

"Thy will be done," is not to be a cry of defeated resignation or an outlet for despair. The petition is not "Thy will be *borne,* or *suffered,*" but "Thy will be *done.*"

Sincerity demands that we be prepared for it to be done first in ourselves. The significance of this petition would be, "Enable us to obey Thy revealed will as fully and as joyously as it is done by the angels in heaven."

We must not forget that in the ultimate, the will of God is a joyous thing. "I delight to do Thy will" (Psalm 40:8). "The cup which the Father has given Me, shall I not drink it? (John 18:11). These are expressions of exultation, not gloomy resignation. The will of God is something positively good to be embraced.

Heaven's music chimes the glad days in,
Hope soars beyond death, pain and sin,
Faith shouts in triumph, Love must win,
Thy will be done.

FREDERICK MANN

Then follow three petitions concerning man and his needs (vv. 11-13). This section covers the essential

needs of man, whether physical, mental, or spiritual, in
the three spheres in which he moves. Bread will meet
his physical needs in the present. Forgiveness for sins
that are past will meet his mental need, for nothing so
disturbs the mind as unpardoned sin. Deliverance from
the tempter's power anticipates his spiritual needs in
the future.

Bread is provided by a loving Father. Forgiveness is
dispensed by the Son. Deliverance and keeping from the
evil one are the prerogative of the Holy Spirit. Thus the
three Persons of the Trinity unite to meet all the physical, mental, and spiritual needs of the believer in the
past, the present, and the future.

Dependence on God's supply. "Give us this day our
daily bread." Although we have our own needs, we are
to be concerned about our needy brothers, and should
ask nothing for ourselves that we do not ask for others.

Bread is referred to as "the staff of life," a staple
necessity. In this context it may well stand for whatever
is necessary for the maintenance of daily life—our temporal needs. "Daily" can here be rendered, "for the
coming day." If we offer the prayer in the morning, it
covers the day already begun. If in the evening, it covers
the following day. The meaning is clear. We are to ask
for God's provision for the immediate future. We are to
live one day at a time, in dependence on His gracious
supply. But man does not live by bread alone. In doing
the will of His Father, Jesus found satisfying food to eat
of which His disciples knew nothing (John 4:32, 34).

Dependence on God's mercy. "Forgive us our debts."
The sense of unforgiven sin and guilt, the sense of
debtorship, creates turmoil in the mind. There is a
hunger of the soul as well as of the body, and it can be
appeased only by forgiveness.

"Debts" here is a Jewish metaphor for sin and is elsewhere so used by Jesus. A debt is an obligation incurred—in this case God has placed upon us an obligation that we have failed to discharge. This obligation embraces sins of omission and of commission. We have robbed both God and man of their due. We need forgiveness, and for this we are entirely dependent on God.

It may be asked, But if my sins were all forgiven when I came to the cross of Christ, why is there need to ask for forgiveness again? The answer is that we live in a polluted and defiling world. Although our sins have been fully forgiven and pardoned in the judicial sense because we have exercised faith in Christ, we do sin after conversion, and for these sins we need forgiveness.

There are two aspects of forgiveness.

1. Judicial forgiveness is granted by God as moral Governor of the universe because of the atonement of Christ. As a result of this forgiveness we "are justified from all things" (Acts 13:39, KJV). God's law now has nothing against us.

2. Paternal forgiveness is bestowed by our Father upon confession of our sins: forgiveness within the family.

Christ's words to Peter illustrate this aspect of forgiveness. When Jesus would wash Peter's feet, he protested: " 'Lord, do You wash my feet? . . . Never shall You wash my feet!' Jesus answered him, 'If I do not wash you, you have no part with Me.' Simon Peter said to Him, 'Lord, not my feet only, but also my hands and my head.' Jesus said to him, 'He who has bathed needs only to wash his feet, but is completely clean' " (John 13:6-10).

Here Jesus makes a distinction between the bathing of the whole body and the washing of the feet; between regeneration and the daily cleansing and forgiveness for defilement contracted in this defiling world. Sin always breaks fellowship and requires forgiveness.

Note too that the petition is not, "Forgive us our debts *because* we forgive others," but *even as* we have forgiven others. The channel of paternal forgiveness is blocked as long as we do not forgive our brothers.

Dependence on God's power. "Do not lead us into temptation, but deliver us from evil [or 'the evil one']" (v. 13, marg.). This is a double-barrelled request. *Temptation* in Scripture is used in two senses. It can mean either "trial, testing," or "incitement to evil." James assures us God never incites to evil (James, 1:13), so in relation to God, the word carries the first meaning, "trial, or testing." God subjects His children to testing to eliminate the dross from the gold in their characters and to strengthen and establish them in holiness. The devil tempts in order to induce them to fall into sin.

So this petition is primarily a prayer for protection in time of testing and danger, when we are open to attacks from the evil one; and secondarily it is a prayer for deliverance when enticed by him to sin.

"Do not lead us into temptation" voices the human shrinking from testings which hold the possibility of failure and falling into sin. "Deliver us from the evil one" is a cry for deliverance in the hour of temptation to evil.

Taken together, the double petition would mean, "Father, spare me this trial, but if in Your wisdom You see it to be necessary for Your glory and my spiritual development, give me the strength to come through it triumphantly and unscathed in the conflict with the evil one." It is, however, a vain exercise to pray, "Do not lead us into temptation," if we voluntarily and unnecessarily place ourselves in situations where we shall find it easy to sin.

The Doxology. "For Thine is the kingdom, and the power, and the glory, forever. Amen."

Although this doxology does not appear in the main manuscripts from which the New Testament is translated, it was used by the Church from very early times. It appears in the Didache, an early Church document of the second century. Although apparently not a part of the prayer as the Lord gave it, it is entirely in keeping with its spirit, and affords a fitting climax of adoration to this, the incomparable prayer.

PRAYER

O Thou who art the only begotten Son, teach us to pray, "Our Father." We thank Thee, Lord, for these living, blessed words which Thou hast given us. We thank Thee for the millions who in them have learnt to know and worship the Father, and for what they have been to us. We look to Thee to lead us deeper into their meaning: do it, we pray Thee, for Thy Name's sake.

ANDREW MURRAY

QUESTIONS

1. How is it possible to retain freshness in a prayer with which we are so familiar?
2. Occasionally check your own prayers to see if you are really following the pattern of prayer the Lord gave.

15

Paul, Man of Prayer

Praying always (Eph 6:18, KJV).

We learn truth best when we see it expressed in a human personality, and this is true of prayer. Of all men of all ages, few, if any, have excelled the apostle Paul in the depth and the effectiveness of their prayer lives. He was at his best in his prayers. In no area of life did he set a more noble and stimulating example. We must be grateful for the self-revelation and insight into prayer with which his letters are studded.

Nowhere does he attempt to explain the possibility or defend the reasonableness of praying. He just takes it for granted and proceeds on the assumption that it is the normal and inevitable function of the regenerate soul, and the natural expression of the spiritual life.

He saw prayer as flowing naturally from the relationship of fatherhood and sonship that exists between God and His children. Because we are sons, He has sent His Spirit into our hearts, as a result of which we cry with great naturalness, "Abba! Father!" (Gal 4:6). This sense of fatherhood provides a rational basis for prayer, for it is perfectly normal for children to have uninhibited intercourse with their father.

To Paul, the supernatural presented no problems. After his own supernatural conversion, anything became possible. To expect the intervention of God in his own affairs and the affairs of men was axiomatic, and he acted consistently with that expectation. He knew no circumstances for which prayer was not appropriate.

In the words of Fleming Stevenson, Paul believed that "prayer is not an arbitrary provision for temporary circumstances, but that it is fixed in the ways of God, and in harmony with the settled relations of the world and the laws of human conduct."[1] Accordingly, it was his conviction that nothing was beyond the reach of prayer except that which was out of the will of God.

Paul's prayers did not just happen. A study of the prayers scattered through Paul's letters will show that they were anything but careless and haphazard. Although they follow no formal pattern, they show clear evidence of careful and reverent thought, and they were doubtless the fruit of much devout meditation as well as the fruit of the Spirit's inspiration. "Study your prayers," said Robert Murray McCheyne. "A great part of my time is spent in getting my heart in tune for prayer."[2]

CHARACTERISTICS OF PAUL'S PRAYERS

Let us note some of the characteristics of Paul's prayers.

1. *They were full of Christ.* It is to this fact that they owe so much of their warmth and stimulating power. An old divine contended that our prayers are so cold and dry because there is so little of Christ in them, a charge that can be laid to all too many prayers, both private and public.

It has been suggested that to stand at Paul's prison door must have been somewhat akin to listening in to our Lord's high priestly prayer in the upper room. What depth of adoration, what height of thanksgiving, what breadth of intercession they express. "Sometimes his whole soul flames up to heaven like incense on the altar fire." Periodically he bursts out into irrepressible doxology of which Christ is the object.

2. *They were unceasing.* I "do not cease giving thanks for you, while making mention of you in my prayers" (Eph 1:16). "Always offering prayer with joy in my every prayer for you all" (Phil 1:4). "For this reason also, since the day we heard of it, we have not ceased to pray for you" (Col 1:9). It may be objected that such language is exaggeration. Perhaps the meaning would be clearer if we used *incessant* instead of "have not ceased." An incessant cough is a constantly recurring cough, and this is the idea behind Paul's statements. These Christians were constantly on his heart, and whenever his mind was free, it naturally turned to prayer for them, as a compass needle turns to the magnetic pole.

Dr. Leon Morris is quoted in *Heart-Cry for Revival:*

> It is not possible for us to spend all our time with the words of prayer on our lips, but it is possible for us to be all our days in the spirit of prayer, realizing our dependence upon God for all that we have and are, realizing something of His presence with us wherever we may be, and yielding ourselves continually to Him for the doing of His will. Where there is such an inward state, it will find outward expression in verbal prayer, and in this connection we should notice the frequent ejaculatory prayers throughout Paul's letters. Prayer was so natural and so continual with the great Apostle that it found its way inevitably into his correspondence.[3]

3. *They were replete with thanksgiving.* He found much material for thanksgiving in those for whom he

prayed. In this he has something important to say to us, for most of us find it much easier to see things with which we can find fault. Typical causes for thanksgiving were the widespread knowledge of the faith of the Roman Christians (Rom 1:8); the enlarged faith and deepening love of the Thessalonians (2 Thess 1:3); the faith, hope, and love of the Colossian believers (Col 1:3-5); and God's deliverance of him from "the body of this death" (Rom 7:24-25).

4. *His prayers were unselfish.* Most of them were concerned with other people and their needs, especially the needs of his converts and the young churches. Intercession was his lifeblood. His prayers for his converts not only evidenced his deep pastoral concern but revealed what he deemed to be their paramount needs. Examples of the qualities and graces he coveted for them were that their love would abound in knowledge (Phil 1:9-11); that they would be filled with the knowledge of His will (Col 1:9-12); that they would prove worthy of their calling (2 Thess 1:11-12); that they would be kept clean from sin (2 Cor 13:7); that they would be united in love and encouraged (Col 2:2). He carried his converts on his heart.

5. *His prayers were affectionate and sincere.* How many of us could say with Paul, "God is my witness, how I long for you all with the affection of Christ Jesus" (Phil 1:8); or, "I have great sorrow and unceasing grief in my heart. For I could wish that I myself were accursed, separated from Christ for the sake of my brethren, my kinsmen according to the flesh" (Rom 9:2-3)?

6. *His prayers were covetous*—in the highest sense. He craved prayer for himself. He was in no sense self-sufficient. He regarded prayer as a joint operation. "You also joining in helping us through your prayers" (2 Cor

1:11). The best remuneration he could receive was the prayer interest of those who had been blessed through his ministry. He saw the prayers of his friends as a determining factor in his service. He asked the Ephesians to pray for bold utterance for him (Eph 6:18-20), and he asked the Colossians to pray for an open door (Col 4:2-4). He asked prayer for deliverance (2 Thess 3:1-2; Philem 22).

7. *His prayers were strenuous.* The words he employed reveal his prayers' true nature. He referred to his prayer for the Colossians as being a conflict, a struggle—"I want you to know how great a struggle I have on your behalf" (Col 2:1). The word here is *agonia.* Elsewhere, it is used of a laboring man at his daily work (Col 1:29); an athlete competing in the arena (1 Cor 9:25); a soldier fighting on the battlefield (1 Tim 6:12). The whole picture is one of intense involvement. He described his prayer as wrestling in Ephesians 6:12 (KJV).

Bishop Handley Moule tells of

> a devoted Sunday schoolteacher who was the means, under God, of bringing scholar after scholar, with always growing frequency, to the feet of Jesus in loving conversion, evidenced by a new life of love and consistency. After her death, her simple diary was found to contain, among other entries, the three following: "'Resolved to pray for each scholar by name.' 'Resolved to wrestle in prayer for each scholar by name.' 'Resolved to wrestle for each by name and to expect an answer.'"[4]

It was thus and without ceasing that Paul prayed.

PRAYER

O God, who through the preaching of the blessed

Apostle Paul hast caused the light of the gospel to shine throughout the world; Grant, we beseech Thee, that we, having his wonderful conversion in remembrance, may show forth our thankfulness to Thee for the same, by following the holy doctrine he taught, through Jesus Christ our Lord.

ANONYMOUS

QUESTIONS

1. From Paul's prayers, make a list of the things he prayed for those for whom he prayed, and follow him in your own intercessions.
2. What was the relation of Paul's secret prayer life to his life of public ministry?

16

Prayer Takes Time

Redeeming the time (Eph 5:16, KJV).

We move on to a lesson that is difficult to master, but which greatly influences the potency of our prayers. Alexander Whyte said,

> I am as certain as I am standing here that the secret of much mischief to our souls, and to the souls of others, lies in the way that we stint, and starve, and scamp our prayers by hurrying over them. Prayer worth calling prayer, prayer that God will call true prayer and will treat as true prayer takes far more time by the clock, than one man in a thousand thinks.[1]

A contemporary of his, Samuel Chadwick, a man of equal spiritual stature, shared the same conviction.

> To pray as God would have us pray is the greatest achievement of earth. Such a life of prayer costs. It takes time. Hurried prayers and muttered Litanies can never produce souls mighty in prayer. Learners give hours regularly every day that they may become proficient in art and mechanism. . . . All praying saints have spent hours every day in prayer. . . . In these days there is no time to pray; but without time, and a lot of it, we shall never learn to pray. It ought to be possible to give God one hour out of twenty-four all to Himself."[2]

Who of us has not experienced the perennial problem of insufficient time for prayer? At least, we tend to excuse ourselves on the grounds that life is so full we do not have sufficient time. But of course it is only an excuse, and not a valid one. Is it not true that each of us can find time for anything he really wants to do? Dr. J. H. Jowett termed the lack-of-time excuse one of the cant phrases of our day. It certainly seems to be on everyone's lips. But let us face it. Is not the lack of urgent desire rather than the lack of adequate time at the root of our meager praying?

William Wilberforce complained, "This perpetual hurry of business and company ruins me in soul if not in body. More solitude and earlier hours! . . . I have been keeping too late hours, and hence have had but a hurried half hour in a morning to myself."[3]

We should honestly face the fact that we each have as much time as the busiest person in the world. The problem is with the way in which we use it. Among other things, the parable of the pounds (Luke 19:11-27) teaches that we have each been entrusted with an equal amount of time, but not all use it so as to produce a maximum return. True, we do not all possess the same capacity, but that fact is recognized in the parable. The reward for the servant with the smaller capacity but equal faithfulness is proportionally the same as that of his more gifted brother. We are not answerable for our capacity, but we are responsible for the strategic use of our time.

If we rate prayer as a high priority in our daily program, we will arrange our day so as to make adequate time for it. The amount of time we allow will be an index of the real importance we attach to it. When our suitcases contain comparatively little, they seem as full as when we carry much, because the less we have, the less meticulously we pack. The man who says he has no time is most likely guilty of careless packing.

What practical steps can be taken to ensure sufficient time for prayer in the daily schedule?

The pressure of motive strongly influences the way in which we use our time. To effect such a radical change in our lifestyle as will make more time for prayer will call for strength of purpose and a deep dependence on the Holy Spirit. Not all of us possess inflexible wills, but even these weak wills of ours can be reinforced, for we can be "strengthened with power through His Spirit in the inner man" (Eph 3:16).

Are there motives sufficiently compelling to cause us to alter the pattern of our lives, to challenge and break long-indulged habits of laxity in the use of time? Indeed there are.

First, and of greatest importance, is the example of our Master. In this as in everything else He is our perfect pattern. He always employed His time strategically, and in selecting His priorities, He always set aside abundant time for prayer. In His pregnant question, "Are there not twelve hours in the day?" (John 11:9), lie the implications of the shortness and yet the sufficiency of time. True, there are *only* twelve hours in the day, but there are *fully* twelve hours in the day—sufficient time to do all the will of God. There is always enough time to do that. Jesus moved in the restful confidence that there was a divine timing for all the events of His life, and He was constantly exercised to keep to His Father's timetable. We may and should follow in His steps.

When Paul urged the Ephesian Christians to redeem the time (Eph 5:16), he was implying that there is a sense in which time is to be bought. It becomes ours by purchase and exchange. There is a price, and sometimes a high price, to be paid for its highest employment.

Henry Martyn of India was a man singularly success-ful in the art of redeeming the time, or, "buying up opportunities," as Henry Alford has it. So urgent did he deem his translation work that he found it impossible to waste an hour. Before his eyes was always the vision of nations waiting for the truth that lay locked up in the Book he was translating. To him, the need of a lost world proved an impelling motive to redeem the hours, and in the brief six years of his meteoric missionary career, he translated the New Testament into three languages.

One practical step that can be taken in order to secure adequate time for prayer is to plug the leaks. We should not think of our day in terms only of hours, but in smaller portions of time, and aim to make constructive use of each of these. Dr. F. B. Meyer, noted preacher and author, packed more into his life than most of his con-temporaries. And his secret? It was said of him that, like John Wesley, he divided his life into periods of five minutes and then endeavored to make each period count for God.

The secret of Charles Darwin's prodigious achieve-ments in the realm of science, it is said, lay in the fact that he knew the difference between ten minutes and a quarter of an hour. How many periods of five, ten, or fifteen minutes that could be devoted to prayer do we waste or leave unemployed in the course of a day? Let us determine to make more and better use of these uncom-mitted but potentially valuable minutes.

An anonymous author likened prayer to the time ex-posure of the soul to God, in which process the image of God is formed on the soul. "We try, in our piety, to practise instantaneous photography. One minute for prayer will give us a vision of the image of God, and we think that is enough. Our pictures are poor because our negative is weak. We do not give God long enough at a sitting to get a good likeness."[4]

"God's acquaintance is not made hurriedly," wrote E. M. Bounds. "He does not bestow His gifts on the casual or hasty comer and goer. To be much alone with God is the secret of knowing Him and of influence with Him."[5]

We should carefully study our priorities in the apportioning of our time each day. Many hours, while not actually wasted, may be spent on matters of only secondary importance. A fool has been defined as one who has lost the proportion of things. Some of us have developed the unfortunate habit of becoming so engrossed in the secondary that there is little time left for the primary. Especially is this the case where prayer is concerned, and our adversary does all in his power to aid and abet.

Check your daily and weekly schedules to see whether you are making adequate time for the essentially spiritual exercises of the soul. See whether the best may not be being relegated to a secondary place by that which is good. Weigh up carefully in the light of eternity the respective values of the opportunities and responsibilities that are claiming your attention. Omit altogether, or give a very minor place to, the things of minor importance. Follow John Wesley's counsel: "Never be unemployed, and never be triflingly employed." And what higher employment can there be than intercourse with the eternal God?

> No time to pray!
> O, who so fraught with earthly care

As not to give a humble prayer
   Some part of day?

No time to pray!
What heart so clean, so pure within,
That needeth not some check from sin,
   Needs not to pray?

No time to pray!
'Mid each day's dangers, what retreat
More needful than the mercy seat?
   Who need not pray?

No time to pray!
Must care or business' urgent call
So press us as to take it all,
   Each passing day?

What thought more drear
Than that our God His face should hide,
And say, through all life's swelling tide,
   No time to hear!

ANONYMOUS

PRAYER

   Eternal God, who by the life of Thy dear Son hast shown us that there is no minute of our own but we may be doing Thy will: Help us to use our time aright, that however we be engaged, in leisure or in play, we may stand before Thee with a pure conscience, acting, speaking, and thinking as in Thy presence, through Jesus Christ our Lord.

ANONYMOUS

QUESTIONS

1. Can we measure the potency of our prayers by their length or brevity?
2. Does God expect everyone to spend the same amount of time in prayer?

17

Exercising Spiritual Authority

I have given you authority (Luke 10:19).

At a conference of missionaries and Chinese pastors held shortly before the Communists gained control of China, one pastor gave a striking address. He said he and his colleagues were more than grateful to those who had brought them the Word of life and the Gospel of Christ. But there was one thing more that they should teach their spiritual children. This new thing was how to pray with authority, so that they might know how to take their stand before the throne of God and rebuke the forces of evil, hold steady, and gain the victory.

The need of teaching on this aspect of prayer is no less pressing in Western lands than in the East. Too few Christians progress from mere presentation of petitions to God into the area of the spiritual warfare of which Paul speaks in Ephesians 6:10-18.

The Spirit-controlled Christian, Paul asserts, is involved in spiritual warfare with powerful but intangible forces. In this conflict only spiritual weapons are effective. But they are available and are "divinely powerful for the destruction of fortresses" (2 Cor 10:4). Of these weapons, the most potent is that recommended by Paul: "pray[er] at all times in the Spirit" (Eph 6:18).

Within the ministry of intercession, there may be contrasting spiritual activity. On the one hand, our prayer may be the calm expression of restful faith: "Ask, and it shall be given to you" (Matt 7:7). On the other hand, it may take the form of intense spiritual conflict: "I want you to know how great a struggle I have on your behalf" (Col 2:1). "Our struggle is not against flesh and blood, but against . . . the spiritual forces of wickedness in the heavenly places" (Eph 6:12). This latter aspect of prayer is known and practiced too little in the life of the Church today.

POWER OVER THE ENEMY'S POWER

Our Lord made a startling statement to His seventy eager disciples, who were elated from the success of their recent evangelistic thrust. Elsewhere Jesus made the claim that all authority, both celestial and terrestrial, had been committed to Him. Here He said to them, "I was watching Satan fall from heaven like lightning. *Behold, I have given you authority . . . over all the power of the enemy*" (Luke 10:18-19, italics added).

The unmistakable inference in this tremendous delegation of spiritual authority to them was that as they exercised that divine authority, they too would see the overthrow of Satan in the area of their own ministry. Nor had they been disappointed. The radiant evangelists could report, "Lord, even the demons are subject to us in Your name" (Luke 10:17).

This promise of spiritual authority over the powers of darkness was never withdrawn, but a little later, when the apostles lost vital faith in Christ's assurance, they found themselves impotent when confronted by a demon-possessed boy (Matt 17:19). It was a failure of their faith, not of the divine promise.

The apostles in this case were paralyzed by their own

unbelief. But after His resurrection, the Master once again affirmed His delegation of authority to them: "By my name they shall expel demons" (Mark 16:17, Weymouth; cf., Luke 10:19).

By His death and resurrection Christ has destroyed (rendered powerless) the devil (Heb 2:14, KJV). As members of His body, we may participate in His victory, and not for ourselves alone, but on behalf of believers in the uttermost parts of the world. Distance is irrelevant in this warfare.

In the record of our Lord's conflict with the carping Pharisees, we are provided with a pictorial representation of what is involved in praying with authority.

The Pharisees had charged Jesus with exorcising demons through the power of the prince of demons. Jesus quickly confronted them with the absurdity of their charge:

> Any kingdom divided against itself is laid waste; . . . and if Satan also is divided against himself, how shall his kingdom stand? . . . But if I cast out demons by the finger of God, then the kingdom of God has come upon you. When a strong man fully armed guards his own homestead, his possessions are undisturbed; but when someone stronger than he attacks him and overpowers him, he takes away from him all his armor on which he had relied, and distributes his plunder" (Luke 11:17-18, 20-22).

The strong man is, of course, Satan, whose power over the minds and spirits of men is mighty though limited. The "stronger than he" (Luke 11:22) is none other than the Lamb, through whose blood we can overcome Satan and all his evil hosts (Rev 12:11).

In the passage quoted above, Christ stated spiritual priorities that are all too often ignored, to the loss of the

Church. He affirmed that if we are ever to plunder Satan's house and deliver his captives, we have a prior responsibility. We must "first bind the strong man" (Matt 12:29, KJV). Have we not often tried to plunder his house without first binding him through the prayer of faith, and then have wondered why we have been turned back in defeat? We have left him unfettered, and he has snatched back souls we have endeavored to rescue from his clutches. Too much of our praying is merely the repeated offering of sincere petitions—and this is of course right—but we fail to do what Jesus said, "First bind the strong man."

In the spiritual warfare in which we should all be engaged, a fierce battle is to be waged. Demons are to be exorcised and the powers of darkness restrained, and sometimes the battle is prolonged. It is a striking fact that it was seven years before Carey baptized his first convert in India. It was seven years before Judson won his first disciple in Burma. Morrison toiled seven years before the first Chinese was brought to Christ; Moffatt waited seven years to see the first movement of the Spirit in Bechuanaland. Henry Richards worked seven years in the Congo before the first convert was gained.[6]

The complete and final defeat of Satan was consummated on the cross, where Jesus triumphed over him in death. Paul interprets the cosmic significance of that decisive conquest for us: "When He had disarmed the rulers and authorities, He made a public display of them, having triumphed over them through Him" (Col 2:15). The purpose of His incarnation was in order that "through death He might render powerless him who had the power of death, that is, the devil" (Heb 2:14).

Any power Satan now exercises over us is either because we fail to apprehend and appropriate the completeness of Christ's triumph, or because we have conceded territory to him through tolerating sin in our lives. In either case, the remedy is clear.

Let us firmly grasp the revealed fact that Jesus has gained a complete and resounding victory over Satan and has robbed him of his power. We have to turn the potential into the actual through the exercise of faith. As members of His body, united to Him by a living faith, we can fully participate in this victory. For the time being and for some wise purpose, which we may not fully understand, he has been allowed limited liberty. But the execution of the sentence already passed on him will be by the hand of Him to whom all judgment has been committed.

In order to exercise this spiritual authority, we must make sure that we are on praying ground and that the indwelling Holy Spirit is ungrieved. We must accept our place of authority as "seated . . . with Him in the heavenly places" (Eph 2:6). It is from this position of authority and power that we can exercise our privilege.

Luke records in Acts 19:13-16 the abortive attempt of some Jewish exorcists, the sons of Sceva, who made use of the name of Jesus in their exorcism of demons. But they were trying to exercise an authority that had never been delegated to them. The formula they adopted in addressing the spirits was, "I adjure you by Jesus whom Paul preaches." But the demon in the possessed man, recognizing the fraud, replied, " 'I recognize Jesus, and I know about Paul, but who are you?' And the man, in whom was the evil spirit, leaped on them and subdued both of them and overpowered them, so that they fled out of that house naked and wounded." It is a solemn thing to lay claim to an authority that has not been delegated to us.

It would be challenging to ask ourselves if our names are known in hell, or if Satan laughs at our puny attempts to plunder his house. Are our prayers effectual in binding the strong man?

Making use of Christ's authority and participating in His victory, we can be influential in binding the strong man in any situation. Only then shall we be in a position to spoil his goods and deliver his captives.

> Blest, when assaulted by the tempter's power,
> The Cross my armour, and the Lamb my Tower,
> Kneeling I triumph—issuing from the fray
> A bleeding conqueror—my life a prey.
>
> ADOLPHE MONOD

PRAYER

Great God, we bless Thee that the battle between Thyself and the powers of darkness has never been uncertain. We praise Thy name that now it is for ever sure to end in victory. Our hearts, amidst the struggles of the present day, would look back to the conflicts of Calvary, and see how our Lord for ever there broke the dragon's head. Oh that Thy people might know that they are contending with a vanquished enemy; that they go forth to fight against one who, with all his subtlety and strength, has·already been overthrown by Him who is our Covenant Head, our Leader, our all.

CHARLES H. SPURGEON

QUESTIONS

1. Does the delegation of spiritual authority to the disciples in our Lord's day (Luke 10:18-19) carry over to our day?
2. Is not the Church greatly handicapping its constituents by failing to teach the aspect of prayer as aggressive spiritual warfare?

18

Power in United Prayer

With one accord (Acts 4:24).

"No great spiritual awakening has begun anywhere in the world apart from united prayer—Christians persistently praying for revival."[1] Such is the dictum of J. Edwin Orr, one of the world's authorities on the subject of revival, and it is a lesson for the Church of our day.

Both Scripture and experience unite to indicate that there is cumulative power in united praying. Faith is infectious, and infection spreads where numbers congregate. Unbelief, on the other hand, thrives more readily in isolation. A single stick can kindle a fire only with great difficulty. Was it not at a united prayer meeting that the power of Pentecost was unleashed?

When a number of Christians unite in prayer for a given person or objective, it is the uniform teaching of Scripture that this brings special spiritual power into operation, for their gathering demonstrates that oneness that God delights to see and acknowledge. Did Jesus not pray, "Holy Father, keep them in Thy name, the name which Thou hast given Me, that they may be one, even as We are" (John 17:11)?

A MODEL PRAYER MEETING

We are introduced to a model meeting for united

prayer in Acts 4:23-31. This historic gathering illus-
trates the effect of united prayer and has valuable lessons for succeeding generations.

So influential had the preaching of the apostles been
that the Jewish leaders sensed a dangerous challenge to
their authority. But because they feared the reactions of
the people who were praising God for what had happened, they refrained from punishing the apostles as
they wished to do. Having gone as far as they dared, they
commanded Peter and John not to speak or teach in the
name of Jesus—a limitation the two men refused to
accept. So after threatening Peter and John further, the
Jewish leaders released them.

The freed men naturally gravitated to their friends,
who were doubtless congregated in the upper room, and
reported their tilt with the hierarchy. Sensing the potential seriousness of the situation, the whole group gave
themselves to prayer. We may learn a great deal from the
content and spirit of their petitions. Note some of the
ingredients that made that meeting so effective.

1. *They were one in heart.* "They lifted their voices to
God with one accord" (v. 24). Prayer thrives where there
is a spirit of love, unity, and fellowship.

2. *They called to mind the majesty and power of the
God to whom they were praying* (v. 24). As they considered the activity of God in creation and providence,
their faith and confidence in Him were strengthened.

3. *They acknowledged the sovereignty of God* in His
power over the nations (vv. 25-28) and confidently expected Him to intervene in their crisis.

4. *They relied on the truthfulness and authority of the
Scriptures* (vv. 25-28). They based their pleas on the
revealed truth of God.

5. *They pled their relationship to Christ,* and sought

that His glory alone would be advanced through the
wonders taking place in His name (v. 30).

6. *They offered specific requests* rather than a general
petition (vv. 29-30):
1. Take note of their threats.
2. Grant Your servants boldness and confidence in
   preaching the Word. In view of the very real danger
   with which they were confronted, they might well
   have asked that they might be excused from preaching. Instead they asked for extra grace and power to
   be able to preach more effectively.
3. Extend Your hand to heal.
4. Give signs and wonders in the name of Your holy
   Servant, Jesus.

7. *Their prayers were answered by a supernatural
demonstration of power.* "The place where they had
gathered together was shaken" (v. 31). God was pleased,
in those early and testing days for His Church, to grant
extraordinary signs to authenticate its supernatural ori-
gin.

8. *They all received the spiritual equipment for which
they prayed.* "They were all filled with the Holy Spirit,
and began to speak the Word of God with boldness"
(v. 31). A new crisis demanded a fresh filling of the
Spirit—a timeless principle. They received exactly
what they asked and believed for.

9. *They directed this fresh enduement of the Spirit
into fresh service* for their Master (vv. 31-35), and their
ministry was with great power.

10. *The united prayer meeting fostered a deeper
spirit of fellowship and sharing.* "Not one of them
claimed that anything belonging to him was his own;
but all things were common property to them" (v. 32).

Powerful prayer meetings such as this are by no

means confined to the apostolic era. Dr. Jonathan Goforth was greatly used by God in revival work in China and Korea. Dr. Walter Phillips described one of his meetings:

> At once on entering one was conscious of something unusual. The place was crowded and tense, reverent attention was on every face. The singing was vibrant with new joy and vigour. People knelt for prayer, silent at first, but soon one and another began to pray aloud. The voices gathered volume and soon blended into a great wave of united supplication that swelled and died down again into an undertone of weeping. Now I understood why the floor was so wet—wet with pools of tears.
>
> Then above the sobbing, in strained choking tones, a man began to make confession. Words of mine would fail to describe the awe and terror and pity of these confessions. It was not so much the enormity of the sins disclosed, or the depths of the iniquity sounded, that shocked one. It was the agony of the penitent, his voice shaken with sobs.

The aftermath of these meetings demonstrated the activity of the Spirit of God in response to the united prayers of His people.

PRAYER

Almighty God, who hast given us grace at this time with one accord to make our common supplications unto Thee, and dost promise that when two or three are gathered together in Thy Name, Thou wilt grant their requests; Fulfil now, O Lord, the desires and petitions of Thy servants, as may be most expedient for them; granting us in this world knowledge of Thy truth, and in the world to come, life everlasting.

CHRYSOSTOM

QUESTIONS

1. What lessons can you learn from the united prayer meeting of Acts 12:1-16?
2. Is united prayer more effectual than the prayer of people praying separately? Can you suggest reasons?

19

World Rulers Need Prayer

Prayers ... for ... all who are in authority (1 Tim 2:1-2).

Prayer for world rulers is enjoined on the praying Christian as a primary responsibility: when counseling his young protégé Timothy, Paul set before him the priorities he should observe.

> First of all, then, [and here it means first in order of importance rather than of time] I urge that entreaties and prayers . . . be made . . . for kings and all who are in authority, in order that we may lead a tranquil and quiet life in all godliness and dignity. This is good and acceptable in the sight of God our Savior" (1 Tim 2:1-3).

The Christian has a civic and national as well as a spiritual responsibility, and among other ways, he is to discharge this responsibility in prayer. He should pray for those who hold civic and national or international offices on all levels. Are we discharging our responsibility in this area? Is it any wonder that the voice of the Church is so muted and her influence so minimal in the councils of the world, when she neglects this primary and divinely ordained method of influencing national and world affairs? If prayer could not so influence the course of world events, Paul's exhortation would be without point.

139

Scripture teaches that the Church and the Christian owe a duty to the state beyond mere payment of taxes and obedience to its laws. It matters not whether rulers are good or bad, we are under obligation to pray for them in their exercise of their offices. In point of fact, the ruler in Rome when Paul penned this letter was the infamous Nero. The king may be a persecutor or a dictator, but Christians are not to stop praying for him.

The early Christians did not evade or ignore their divinely imposed civic and national responsibilities. One of the early Fathers, Tertullian, affords us a glimpse into their practice: "We pray for ourselves, for the state of the world, for the peace of all things, and for the postponement of the end."

Men in public office have heavy burdens to bear, and they wield far-reaching influence. Their decisions affect the Church, the city, and the nation. The hands of wicked men and corrupt officials can be stayed by our prayers.

In the midst of toppling thrones, Daniel maintained his serenity because he knew there was a sovereign God in heaven to whom he could pray. For him, that canceled every adverse factor. He could defy the decree of the Oriental despot, for he knew that "the Most High is ruler over the realm of mankind, and bestows it on whom He wishes" (Dan 4:17).

The purpose of such prayer, says Paul, is that leaders may be led aright and that our lives may be lived aright. We are encouraged to pray for times of peace, not merely that we might enjoy lives of ease and comfort, but that there should be the minimum of disturbance so as to facilitate the spread of the Gospel.

God fervently desires that all men shall be saved and

come to the knowledge of the truth (1 Tim 2:4). If this is to be brought about, the type of government under which they live will have an important bearing. The cases of China and Soviet Russia are poignant examples of this. Although the Church cannot be stamped out in Communist-controlled lands, the opportunity for men and women to hear and accept the Gospel is drastically curtailed.

This passage assures us, too, that it is acceptable to ask God that we may live a tranquil and quiet life, free from disturbance from without and perturbation from within, in order that the Gospel be not hindered.

In offering such prayer, we must bear in mind the sobering fact that even earnest prayer cannot avert the righteous judgment of God on men or nations when their cup of iniquity is full. But as we pray, we can be confident that as the result of the prayers of the Church, God will answer in a way that will be in the best interests of His creatures and will be consistent with His nature and attributes.

PRAYER

Give us new hearts, and renew Thy Holy Spirit within us, O Lord; that our rulers may faithfully minister justice, punish sin, defend and maintain the preaching of Thy Word, and that all ministers may diligently teach Thy dearly beloved flock purchased by the blood and death of Thine own and only dear Son our Lord, and that all people may obediently learn and follow Thy law, to the glory of Thy holy name for Christ's sake, our only Lord and Saviour.

JAMES PILKINGTON

QUESTIONS

1. In praying for matters of national and international importance, do we really expect our prayers to achieve something definite?
2. What motives should influence Christians in totalitarian lands to pray for rulers who are tyrannical and cruel?

20

Should Christians Fast?

When you fast (Matt 6:17).

Prayer and fasting are linked together both in the Scriptures and in the life-patterns of many saints of God. But fasting, in the sense in which the New Testament uses the word, has gone out of fashion. "Fasting of the mind," or "fasting of the spirit" is advocated rather than abstinence from food. But to be consistent, might we not just as well talk of giving alms in the spirit? There is little doubt that in their usage of the word, the biblical writers had in mind the partial or complete abstinence from food for a period for a religious purpose.

There may be some ground for widening its application, however, provided we do not lose sight of its basic significance. For example, the saintly Andrew Bonar contended that fasting is abstaining from all that hinders prayer. Himself an avid reader, he had at times to fast from his overweening love of reading to make time for communion with God. Phillips Brooks regarded fasting as the voluntary disuse of anything innocent in itself, with a view to spiritual culture. Some may find it necessary to fast from some social pleasures for the same reason.

NOT A RITE OF THE KINGDOM

It is noteworthy that although our Lord fasted at times, as during the temptation in the wilderness (Matt 4:2), and although He instructed His disciples as to the spirit in which fasting is to be undertaken (Matt 6:16-18), He refrained from appointing any fast as a rite of His Kingdom (Matt 9:14-17; 11:18-19). While not disapproving of or abolishing the practice of fasting, Jesus lifted it out of the strait jacket of Old Covenant legalism into the liberty of the New.

Jesus Himself doubtless observed all the prescribed Jewish fasts, but in all His teaching He spoke of fasting only twice. Indeed, so little an ascetic was He in His lifestyle that they laid the charge against Him—utterly unfounded, of course—of being a glutton and drunkard. Nowhere did He make fasting obligatory.

When the disciples of John asked Jesus, "Why do we and the Pharisees fast, but Your disciples do not fast?" (Matt 9:14), His reply was that since fasting was a sign of mourning, it would be inappropriate to engage in it while He as Messiah and Bridegroom was with them (Matt 9:14-17). The time would come when He would be removed from them. Then it would not be inconsistent to fast. But it should be noted that He left the question open. (Textual scholars consider "fasting" in Matthew 17:21 and Mark 9:29, marg., to be corruptions of the text.)

There are only four indisputable references to voluntary fasting in the New Testament. In addition to the two that have been cited, there are two in the book of Acts—13:2 and 14:23. The references in 2 Corinthians 6:5 and 11:27 seem to have involuntary fasting in view.

In a penetrating study of the subject of voluntary fasting, Dr. Henry W. Frost asserts that it is nowhere enjoined on the Christian as a duty.[1] We may or may not fast, as we choose. David Livingstone had very definite views on the subject. "Fastings and vigils without a special object in view are time run to waste. They are made to minister to a sort of self-gratification, instead of being turned to good account."[2]

A SPONTANEOUS REACTION

Fasting is not a legalistic requirement but a spontaneous reaction under special circumstances. Some, like Luther, Whitefield, Edwards, Brainerd, and Martyn, found it a spiritually rewarding practice. There are other godly and prayerful people who have found fasting a hindrance rather than a help. Some are so constituted physically that the lack of a minimum amount of food renders them unable to concentrate in prayer.

There is no need for such to be in bondage. Let them do what most helps them to pray. Dr. O. Hallesby observes, "Fasting is an outward act which should be carried out only when there is an inner need of it."[3]

The idea that food produces carnality, whereas abstinence from food induces spirituality, is without biblical warrant. It is true that overindulgence in food is not conducive to deep spirituality, but that is another matter. It was Paul's teaching that "the kingdom of God is not eating and drinking, but righteousness and peace and joy in the Holy Spirit" (Rom 14:17). He said further, "But food will not commend us to God; we are neither the worse if we do not eat, nor the better if we do eat" (1 Cor 8:8). Clearly, fasting is a matter in which there is complete liberty.

The two occasions recorded in the Acts on which fasting is mentioned as being practiced are when Paul and Barnabas were being set apart for missionary work

(13:2-3) and when the two men appointed elders to the churches that had resulted from their endeavors (14:23).

The teaching of Scripture appears to be not that fasting is a carnal means of attaining a spiritual end, but rather that it is the outcome of preoccupation with matters of overriding importance. Dr. Frost points out that in the New Testament, fasting is nowhere the result of premeditation, nor is it predetermined or prearranged. Historically, it was usually associated with some strong emotion created by some deep and special spiritual concern.[4]

This would undoubtedly be the case in our Lord's temptation (Matt 4:2). If the reference to fasting in Acts 10:30-31, KJV, is really in the original text, there is little doubt of the deep concern that led Cornelius to beseech God for clearer revelation of His truth. It is also clear that the leaders of the church at Antioch were heavily burdened with their responsibility to spread the Gospel to a lost world, since God answered their prayers by thrusting out two of their members who could least be spared to initiate the missionary enterprise. No less a burden would be on the spirits of Saul and Barnabas when they appointed the elders on whom the whole future of the young churches would depend.

AN OVERMASTERING CONCERN

In the grip of an overmastering concern, these men were led to a prolongation of prayer which precluded partaking of food. To them, praying was of greater importance than eating. The length of the fast was determined not so much by a previous resolution but by the pressure of heart concern. When the burden lifted, the fasting automatically ceased. Its purpose had been achieved.

The conclusion would seem to be that fasting after the New Testament pattern was the spontaneous outcome of (1) the challenge of a special test or temptation; or (2) a deep yearning after a closer walk with God; or (3) a heavy burden for the spread of the Gospel in the regions beyond; or (4) spiritual travail for the upbuilding of the church; or (5) the exigencies of a stubborn situation.

"These subjects are connected with a large spiritual development," wrote Dr. Frost, "and it will be only the highly spiritual man who will be so occupied with them as to count them more necessary than his meat and drink."[5]

One obvious value of fasting lies in the fact that its discipline helps us keep the body in its place. It is a practical acknowledgment of the supremacy of the spiritual. But in addition to this reflex value, fasting has direct benefits in relation to prayer as well. Many who practice it from right motives and in order to give themselves more unreservedly to prayer testify that the mind becomes unusually clear and vigorous. There are a noticeable spiritual quickening and increased power of concentration on the things of the spirit.

Pastor Hsi, a noted Chinese scholar-saint, demonstrated the value of fasting and prayer in his most remarkable ministry. "Constantly and in everything he dealt with God," wrote a fellow traveler.

> In a very real way he dealt with Satan too. His conflict with the Evil One at times was such that he would give himself to days of fasting and prayer. Even when travelling, I have known him fast for a whole day over some difficult matter that needed clearing up. That was always his resource, fasting and prayer. I have never seen such influence over others. . . . I was profoundly interested in his spirituality and earnestness; his prayers

and fastings; the intensity of his purpose—nothing in the world but the one thing.[6]

In the early days of the China Inland Mission, Dr. J. Hudson Taylor and his colleagues had reached the decision to ask God for seventy new missionaries—an almost unprecedented missionary petition in 1881. With a group of fellow missionaries, a day of united prayer and fasting was held. "On the morning of our fast day," wrote one participant, "the Holy Spirit seemed so to fill several of us, that each felt (as we found in private conversation afterwards) that we could not bear any more and live."[7] The subjective blessing that was experienced by those who prayed was not the only result. God answered their prayers and gave the seventy workers.

PRAYER

O Lord, who for our sake didst fast forty days and forty nights, give us grace to use such abstinence that, our flesh being subdued to the spirit, we may ever obey Thy godly motions in righteousness, and true holiness, to Thy honour and glory, who livest and reignest with the Father and the Holy Spirit, one God, world without end.

ANONYMOUS

QUESTIONS

1. Is there spiritual merit in fasting, or is its value only in the discipline involved?
2. Why do you think Jesus did not introduce fasting in the manifesto of His Kingdom?

21

Praying for Missionaries

Pray ye therefore the Lord of the harvest
(Matt 9:38, KJV).

"Brethren, pray for us that the word of the Lord may spread rapidly and be glorified" (2 Thess 3:1). This moving plea from the first and greatest missionary, whose great gifts and spiritual endowment may well have made him less dependent than others, indicates the importance he laid on the intercessions of his friends. Note in the following verses the juxtaposition of the hard-pressed missionary's extremity with the part he expected intercession to play in his deliverance. "We were burdened excessively, beyond our strength, so that we despaired even of life . . . , [but God] delivered us . . . , you also joining in helping us through your prayers" (2 Cor 1:8-11). He believed intercession could be instrumental in delivering missionaries from the plotting of their enemies and opponents. "Finally, brethren, pray for us . . . , that we may be delivered from perverse and evil men" (2 Thess 3:1-2). He believed that closed doors could be made to swing open on their hinges as urgent prayer was made to God. "Praying at the same time for us as well, that God may open up to us a door for the word" (Col 4:3).

As Northcote Deck wrote:

149

What benison, what benediction would you bestow on isolated missionaries through your prayers? There is nothing more profitable, more priceless that you can ask for us than that, in spite of physical weariness and infirmities and the care of many churches and multiplying converts, *we may be enabled to remain on our knees.* For there is a praying in detail that has to be done if infant churches are to grow and prosper. And this detailed praying can be done only by those on the field. Only we know the names, the lives, the temptations of the converts.... And we? We fall asleep upon our knees!... But we earnestly desire "through your prayers and the provision of the Spirit of Jesus Christ," that we might be given enough spiritual energy to make full proof of this vital ministry. But we need your help.[1]

This plea from a veteran missionary is an echo of that of Paul, and it is re-echoed from thousands of hearts around the world.

REASONS FOR DEPENDENCE ON PRAYER

Because you prayed—
God touched our weary bodies with His power
And gave us strength for many a trying hour
In which we might have faltered, had not you,
Our intercessors, faithful been and true.

CHARLES B. BOWSER

The question might well be asked: Why are missionaries so dependent on the prayers of friends in the home churches? The following reasons may be advanced:

1. God has placed the missionary enterprise on a prayer basis. This is God's method of working to achieve His worldwide purpose. For example, Jesus taught us to "beseech the Lord of the harvest to send out workers

into His harvest" (Matt 9:38). He taught also that success in spiritual work is the outcome of prevailing prayer.

2. We are members of the body of Christ, and each member is dependent on the other members. God does not intend us to operate independently or in isolation.

3. The very nature of missionary work makes prayer essential. Our representatives in the front lines are not primarily overcoming cultural prejudices and superstitions, but are engaged in hand-to-hand conflict with the prince of this world and his followers. It requires spiritual weapons to overcome an invisible spiritual foe, and prayer is the weapon God has provided (Eph 6:12, 18).

It has been pointed out that in this spiritual warfare, the Lord refused to deal with flesh and blood, or with the secular powers of His time. His one objective was to deal with the spiritual forces behind the evils around Him. In the woman with a spirit of infirmity, He saw not merely a disease, but satanic bondage. He described her as the woman "whom Satan has bound" (Luke 13:16). To the woman, He said not, "You are *healed*," but, "You are *freed* from your sickness" (Luke 13:12, italics added).

Behind every idol there lurks an evil spirit, and this explains the implacable hostility of God to idolatry in every form. The missionary task is to deal with this enemy through intercession based on the victory of Calvary, and thus free the captives.

4. The missionary is very human in his reactions to testing circumstances such as loneliness, climatic conditions, unfamiliar culture, linguistic limitations, absence of stimulating Christian ministry and fellowship, discouragement, separation from home and loved ones, plus the incidental pressures of the work. This factor makes the prayers of friends doubly necessary.

Not all missionary situations impose great strains, but

the missionary calling lays one open to many more of these than would be the case in a normal situation at home.

In *Archibald the Arctic*, Bishop Fleming states that throughout the whole of his missionary career in the Arctic, he was always cold, always hungry, always lonely. What blessing and support prayer can bring to such valiant souls working under such conditions.

5. Missionaries are usually greatly in the minority and tend to be overwhelmed by the magnitude of the task. They need the reinforcement of prayer support from the home base.

Joshua and his army were down in the plain, locked in battle with the ruthless Amalekites. On the hill was Moses with his two lieutenants, Aaron and Hur. Moses was engaged in intercession, of which his uplifted rod was the symbol. There was no obvious connection between the two groups. Moses was far removed from the tangible enemies, yet it was he who, through prayer, controlled the swaying tides of battle (Exod 17:8-13).

The poet Cowper captures the story in four lines:

> When Moses stood with arms spread wide,
> Success was found on Israel's side.
> But when through weariness they failed,
> That moment Amalek prevailed.

In the fluctuating battle, the key to victory lay in the hands of the three octogenarians (an encouragement to old believers who are no longer fit for front-line service). Not arms, but the weaponless hands of prayer, controlled the issue. The seeming inactivity of prayer on the hill proved to be a greater test of spiritual stamina than fighting in the valley. It was Moses who tired, not Joshua.

The incident teaches us, too, that there is a cumulative effect in prayer. The focusing of many prayers on one life or on a situation can change defeat into victory.

How should we go about the work of intercession for missions so as to make the maximum contribution? Some suggestions follow for those who desire to become effective intercessors.

1. First and foremost, make a firm resolve and deliberate decision, not without first counting the cost, to set aside time for regular intercession. Let only the most urgent happening break into this routine.

2. Ask the Lord to guide you to a special field of interest. Gather all the information you can, and take an intelligent interest in a few missionaries and missionary situations. Endeavor to become literate in missionary matters.

3. Seek a personal link with some missionary for whom you can exercise a special prayer ministry as a prayer companion. Correspond with him and follow details of the work in prayer. Experience will enlarge your interests and guide your intercessions.

4. Have a prayer list in which you note the names of missionaries, perhaps praying for different continents on different days of the week. Scripture Gift Mission issues a helpful booklet, *The Remembrancer*, as a help to systematizing the prayer life.

5. Obtain literature on the places for which you desire to pray so that you have an intelligent grasp of strategic points on which to focus prayer. Learn what you can about the national people, leaders, and churches.

6. Do not become discouraged if results in the work for which you are praying seem meager. Is that not really a reason for praying more earnestly?

7. Leave yourself open to God for Him to lay special prayer burdens on your heart. Such prayers can be mightily effectual.

FOR WHAT SHOULD WE PRAY SPECIFICALLY?

It has been asserted that there has never been a significant outpouring of the Spirit on the mission field without the previous outpouring of the human spirit to God in prayer. Every new Pentecost has had a preparatory period of burdened supplication.

Our prayers should be strategic and focused, dealing with the great central issues involved in the missionary enterprise as well as with the personal details of the missionary and his needs. Too often we are mainly occupied with trifling issues that are at the circumference, while major issues are neglected. A balance should be found. Here are a few strategic subjects:

1. That spiritual revival and quickening may come to the national churches, and especially to the key leaders.

2. That international affairs may be so overruled that the work of the Gospel may not be hindered. Satan is working very powerfully in the political realm, but Paul encourages us to believe that the prayers of God's people can significantly influence the course of world events from the prayer room.

3. That unresponsive individuals and groups may experience deep conviction of sin and respond to the Gospel. There are certain places where the adversary has a stronger grip on the hearts of the people than in others, e.g., Pergamum is spoken of as the place "where Satan's throne is" (Rev 2:12-13). Only persistent prayer can wear down this opposition.

> Because you prayed—
> God touched our lips with coals of fire,
> Gave Spirit-fulness and did so inspire
> That, when we spoke, sin-blinded souls did see;
> Sin's chains were broken;
> Captives were made free.
>
> CHARLES B. BOWSER

4. That the spiritual tone of missions and missionaries may be kept high, and that their policies may be sufficiently flexible to meet rapidly changing conditions.
5. That national leaders may be gripped by the vision of their churches reproducing themselves and reaching out across cultural boundaries into the regions beyond.
6. That the home churches may increasingly rise to their responsibilities in prayer, support, and reinforcement.
7. That God would thrust out new workers to maintain and extend the work.

PRAYING FOR PERSONAL NEEDS

There is, in addition to what we could call strategic praying, the necessity to pray for the personal needs of the workers whom we send out. Elsie Purnell has written an article concerning the problems facing the missionary mother, for whom prayer is needed.[2] If we are to pray for such with insight and feeling, we should endeavor to think ourselves into their position and pray accordingly.

According to the article, "Many a missionary mother is frustrated over the conflict in her mind between her duties to her family and to 'the work . . . .' She can find a multitude of Scriptures about her duties as wife and

mother, but none specifically about a mother involved
in missionary work." What priorities is she to observe?
Must one be sacrificed for the other? "Pray that the
missionary mothers on your prayer list will be able to
resolve this conflict and feel satisfied."

The missionary woman is often facing financial problems. On furlough she will fit into the low-income
bracket. She will not have the things her friends and
family and neighbors have. Pray that she will learn to
adjust to this situation, and that her feelings about material things will not drain her emotional strength.

Loneliness can be an almost devastating problem,
especially for the single woman. The article has this to
say concerning the test the single woman faces: "While
rarely discussed publicly, singleness can be the greatest
problem facing some women overseas. Some single
missionaries are happy and satisfied; others have recurring questions and battles." Pray that they may find a
solution to this problem in the more deeply realized
presence of Christ with them.

Separation from children is probably the most
traumatic of all the testing experiences that come to
missionary mothers. If ever they need prayer support, it
is when the parting days come. Pray that they will know
God's peace and grace abundantly at this time.

If you are aware that a missionary has to face problems
among his folks at home—problems such as serious
illness, bereavement, breakup of marriage, children
going astray—uphold him as he carries these added
burdens.

PRAYER FOR PHYSICAL SAFETY

Prayer for the physical safety of missionaries is always appropriate and appreciated. There are endless

testimonies of remarkable answers to such prayers for safekeeping. Here is one.

> One night at midnight Mrs Ed. Spahr was awakened and burdened for missionary friends Rev. Jerry and Mrs Rose in Dutch New Guinea (now Irian Jaya) working among stone-age culture people. She was so burdened for him she prayed and next morning wrote a letter telling of it. Later it was learned that he received prayer letters from five prayer partners in five continents saying they prayed for him on that specific occasion.
>
> By adjusting the dateline and time span it was seen that they all prayed at the same time—at that very time Mr Rose was standing with his arms tied behind his back and a huge "stone-age" savage standing before him with a spear ready to pin him to the ground.
>
> As five prayer partners on five continents prayed, another man in the tribe (there were no Christians in the tribe at the time) spoke to the man and he walked away. Dr Spahr asks: "Could God have made him walk away without the prayer partners? God can do anything he wills, but would he? I don't think he would have. I think it was His desire and will to continue the life of Jerry Rose on earth as a witness through his prayer partners."[3]

Paul the intercessor admits us into the secrets of his own special burdens in the prayers he offers for the churches that were the outgrowth of missionary work. They were very like churches in missionary lands today.

"I want you to know," he wrote, "how great a struggle [*agonia*] I have on your behalf, and for those who are at Laodicea, and for all those who have not personally seen my face" (Col 2:1). This brings him alongside us; for, like him, we must often pray for people whom we have never seen.

STRATEGIC PRAYING

It is instructive to notice the things he asked for these young churches (Col 2:2) so that we can imitate him. He was not concerned for trivialities, but for deep spiritual needs. He asked (1) for *spiritual strengthening,* "that their hearts may be encouraged"; (2) for *spiritual unity,* "having been knit together in love"; (3) for *spiritual certitude,* "attaining to all the wealth that comes from the full assurance of understanding"; (4) for *spiritual insight,* "resulting in a true knowledge of God's mystery, that is, Christ Himself." This is the crowning point of the prayer, for in the full knowledge of Christ, everything else is included.

The same letter introduces us to another mighty intercessor, Epaphras. "I do not know that Epaphras was an eloquent preacher," said Joseph Parker, "but he was mighty in intercession. He threw his arms around his native church and toiled in prayer for them until his brow was bedewed with agony, and his whole face was lighted up with saintly expectation that he might see the descending blessing."

He drew this picture from the brief glimpse Paul gives in Colossians 4:12. "Epaphras . . . sends you his greetings, always laboring earnestly [*agonizomenos*] for you in his prayers, that you may stand perfect and fully assured in all the will of God." Prison walls could not restrain the flight and freedom of the soul of this concerned pastor. Denied personal contact with his flock, he could still exercise on their behalf the most potent of all ministries. His concern for their spiritual advancement found expression in prayer that amounted almost to agony, for that is the word used. This was no mere passive and benevolent well-wishing. He took his praying seriously. The picture behind the word is that of a perspiring wrestler straining every muscle.

What a pale reflection of this are our tepid and languid prayers! How little most of us know of this conflict, this laboring, this travail in prayer that characterized the praying of these two men of God and has been repeated in the lives of many choice souls down the ages!

PRAYER

O God of all the nations of the earth, remember the multitudes of the heathen, who, though created in Thine image, have not known Thee, nor the dying of Thy Son their Saviour Jesus Christ; and grant that by the prayers and labours of Thy holy Church they may be delivered from all ignorance and unbelief, and brought to worship Thee; through Him whom Thou hast sent to be the Resurrection and the Life of all men, Thy Son Jesus Christ our Lord.

FRANCIS XAVIER

QUESTIONS

1. See if you can match the prayers of Paul's friends for him with actual answers.
2. Do you have a regular and systematic place in your prayers for missionary work?

22

Prayer and Revival

If my people . . . shall . . . , I . . . will
(2 Chron 7:14, KJV).

"Oh, that you would burst forth from the skies and come down! How the mountains would quake in your presence! The consuming fire of your glory would burn down the forests and boil the oceans dry. The nations would tremble before you; then your enemies would learn the reason for your fame! So it was before when you came down, for you did awesome things beyond our highest expectations, and how the mountains quaked!" (Isa 64:1-3, TLB).

The poet Burns spoke of "Rapt Isaiah's wild seraphic fire," and the above paragraph is aflame with it. In the vocative plea of this majestic passage, one can sense the fire burning in Isaiah's heart. In vivid phrase and with moving eloquence, he pours out his heart to God, pleading for a divine visitation on his needy nation. It is a poignant, almost desperate prayer, but laced with ardent faith.

In verse seven, Isaiah gives what Samuel M. Zwemer described as an incomparable definition of prayer: "There is no one who calls on Thy name, who arouses himself *to take hold of Thee*" (italics added). What a vivid picture. "The suppliant stirs himself out of lethargy and sleep to seize hold of God, and he says, 'I will not let you go except You bless me and answer my prayer'". [1] This is the kind of praying that opens the windows of heaven. There is no tepidity here—intellect, emotions, and will unite to take hold of God.

In chapter sixty-three, verse fifteen, Isaiah cries, "O Lord, *look down* from heaven and see us" (TLB, italics added). He pleads, "Oh, that you would burst forth from the skies and *come down!*" (Isa 64:1, TLB, italics added). He recalls the wonders of Sinai (64:3-4) and asks for a repetition of the supernatural intervention. Then he pours out his heart in confession. "We are all infected and impure with sin. When we put on our prized robes of righteousness we find they are but filthy rags.... And our sins, like the wind, sweep us away. Yet no one calls upon your name" (64:6-7, TLB).

The nation had reached the state at which only an invasion from heaven could meet their desperate need, for they faced a dual problem—closed heavens and an absent God. Isaiah had exhausted his own repertoire; he had no prescription for the national malady. Only God could meet the situation.

So Isaiah was very bold (Rom 10:20) and said in effect, "If no one else will take hold of God, I shall. Oh, that You would come down and display Your mighty power!" Have we reached the stage of desperation yet, or have we opted for a continuance of the status quo? Is this not what we need for our powerless churches and sick and decadent society?

Around 1950, there was a powerful movement of the Spirit in the Hebrides. The awakening did not just happen. For some months, a number of men met three nights a week for prayer; they often spent hours. The weeks passed and nothing happened until one morning at about two o'clock; a young man read Psalm 24:3-5,

"Who may stand in His holy place? He who has clean hands and a pure heart, who has not lifted up his soul to falsehood, and has not sworn deceitfully. He shall receive a blessing from the LORD."

> [He] closed the Bible and looking at his companions on their knees before God, he cried: "Brethren, it is just so much humbug to be waiting thus night after night, month after month, if we ourselves are not right with God. I must ask myself—'Is my heart pure? Are my hands clean?'" And at that moment, . . . something happened. God swept into that prayer group and at that wonderful moment seven Elders discovered what they evidently had not discovered before, that revival must be related to Holiness . . . . They found themselves in the searching power of the presence of God and discovered things about themselves they had never suspected. But the Blood of Calvary heals and cleanses . . . . These men . . . found themselves lifted to the realm of the supernatural. These men knew that Revival had come.[2]

This was the beginning of a movement that went from congregation to congregation and island to island off the coast of Scotland, with far-reaching effects.

Some other instances of the power of prevailing prayer follow. The author presents these examples of prayer that is accompanied by a cleansing of heart and life and results in powerful spiritual revival, in the hope that faith and aspiration will be kindled in the hearts of readers.

> A young married woman [Mary Binnie, who in her later years was known to the author and whose granddaughter became his wife] . . . had been converted in the Great Revival of 1859. [She] was a member of Charlotte Baptist Chapel in Edinburgh. Although this church had a noble history, it had fallen on evil days. Her heart was

deeply burdened at the spiritual state of the church, and as she prayed, she received the clear conviction, from the Spirit of God she believed, that it was His purpose to send revival to the moribund Charlotte Chapel. She gave herself to prayer, and expectantly awaited the answer, little dreaming how many years would elapse before the promised revival came, or what was to be her part in it.

Then tragedy struck. Her husband was suddenly taken from her side, leaving her with three small children, and twins which were born shortly after his death. As she had few financial resources, her mother who lived in Kelso urged her to live with her. This she was loath to do as she felt she must be there when the revival came to the Chapel. At last circumstances compelled her to accept her mother's invitation, and she took her little family to Kelso, but her intercessions for the revival were as urgent as ever.

At that time Kelso could boast no Baptist Chapel, so she set herself to pray that someone would be moved to build one. One day while walking down the main street of the town she was accosted by a wealthy lady who, in the course of conversation told her that God had laid it on her heart to build a Baptist Chapel in Kelso! The startling announcement did not at all surprise this woman of faith who had implicit confidence in the power of God to answer prayer.[3]

When the chapel was built, they called a young man recently graduated from the Glasgow Bible Institute, Joseph W. Kemp. Under his vigorous ministry the church prospered, and in due course he married one of the twin daughters of the godly widow.

But what of the promised revival at Charlotte Chapel? Through the intervening years "the importunate widow" had "not staggered at the promise of God through unbelief," but had persistently pressed her suit

at the throne of grace. It takes little imagination to picture her awe when an invitation came to her loved son-
in-law to occupy the vacant pulpit of Charlotte Chapel.
Was God at last going to answer the prayers of many
years? Was He going to send revival, using as His in-
struments her own daughter and her husband? Then the
long test of faith had been abundantly worth-while.

From the moment of the advent of the energetic young
pastor, the tide in the affairs of the church turned deci-
sively. The congregation of thirty-five at the welcome
meeting quickly began to increase under the persua-
siveness of his passionate preaching.

His life-long tendency to overwork began to affect Mr.
Kemp's health and his officers suggested a holiday, but
he spent it visiting the Welsh Revival which was then at
its height. There he saw scenes enacted before his eyes
that filled him with a longing to see a similar movement
of the Spirit in his own church.

On returning to Edinburgh, he shared his burden with
some members of his church who were gathered in
prayer. From that moment the flood-gates of blessing
were opened wide. Night after night, week after week
the meetings increased in numbers and intensity.[4]

One who was reporting on the movement wrote:

It is impossible to convey any adequate idea of the
prayer passion that characterised those meetings. There
was little or no preaching, it being no uncommon experience for the pastor to go to the pulpit on the Lord's
Day and find the congregation so caught in the spirit of
prayer as to render preaching out of the question. For a
whole year the church prayed on night by night without
a single break.

The people poured out their hearts in importunate
prayer. I have yet to witness a movement that has produced more permanent results in the lives of men,
women and children. There were irregularities, no

doubt; some commotion, yes. There was that which shot itself through all prescribed forms and shattered all conventionality. But such a movement with all its irregularities is to be preferred far above the dull, dreary, monotonous decorum of many churches. Under these influences, crowds thronged the chapel which, only three years before, maintained a sombre vacuum.[5]

Writing of the movement, the pastor said that during the first year he had personally dealt with no fewer than one thousand souls who had been brought to God during the prayer meetings. Conversions took place at every meeting.

"At the end of the first year of this sovereign visitation, . . . it seemed as though the tide of spiritual fervour was on the ebb. The pastor made preparation for a course of teaching with a view to consolidating and conserving the wonderful work of the past year. But once again the Spirit of God intervened."[6]

At a late prayer meeting, the fire of God fell. There was nothing, humanly speaking, to account for what happened. Quite suddenly upon one and another came an overwhelming sense of the reality and awfulness of His presence and of eternal things. Life, death and eternity seemed suddenly laid bare. Prayer and weeping began, and gained in intensity every moment. One was overwhelmed before the sudden bursting of the bounds. Could it be real? The midnight hour was reached. The hours had passed like minutes.[7]

The revival fires blazed for a second whole year, during which eight hundred more sought and found the Lord in the chapel. One elder wrote of the prayer meetings,

It has been my privilege to be at some of the wonderful

early and late prayer meetings which have been such a
marked feature of the revival. He has attended half
nights of prayer and whole nights of prayer, some of
which will never be forgotten; but in no case has he ever
seen anything like what has taken place in the past few
weeks.

Here were men and women on their knees, many filled
with an intense passionate longing, with strong crying
to God; others in bondage yet longing to be free; some
melted by love divine, whose eyes with tears o'erflowed.
At times the spirit of prayer so increased that it seemed
as if all were praying. At another time the soul gave vent
in song as it overflowed in joy. The sense of God's
nearness and presence was at times overwhelming.[8]

This extended account is given, first, to kindle desire
and stimulate prayer that there might be a similar quickening in our own times; second, to show the power and
effectiveness of the prayers of one obscure saint whose
name never hit the headlines, but whose name is held in
high honor in heaven.

Not long before China fell to the Communists, the
author was privileged to visit the Chungking Theologi-
cal Seminary with a colleague, Fred Mitchell, Chairman
of the English Keswick Convention; each delivered several messages to the student body.

The principal of the seminary, the Reverend Marcus
Cheng, and the students had for some time been praying
that showers of blessing might fall on their hungry
hearts. The principal wrote:

In describing the experience, I would say, "then the
fire of the Lord fell." The Holy Spirit was in control, and
although the speakers were several, the theme was one,
and the messages related to one another in such a way
that there was a progression of thought.

The Holy Spirit began to convict of sin. All our consciences were quickened, causing the remembrance of hidden and forgotten sins. The light of the Holy Spirit penetrated the inmost recesses of the heart so that we could not but repent, making confession in public prayer and spontaneous grief and tears. At each meeting, after the close of the message, one after another in rapid succession stood up and prayed for an hour or two. Even then the meeting would have carried on indefinitely had we allowed it to do so.

Classes were suspended for a week that every one might have the opportunity of waiting on God. The Spirit of prayer truly came upon us. Moreover, all general terms and hackneyed expressions were discarded and requests were specific. "Lord, forgive me this sin," (naming it). Some confessed many many sins, one after another. We came to have a genuine hatred of sin.

Not only was confession made to God and man, but as far as possible each made apology and restitution. Apart from monetary restitution there was one who produced articles that did not belong to him, a hat and a torch. One confessed that he had failed to tithe and gave a gold ring. Another said, "I have sinned against so and so who is now dead. How can I apologize now?" Nearly every student felt he had to write letters to family or friends making confession or testifying. Two afternoons were given over to writing such letters. One wrote thirty. Stationery and stamps became a problem. Just then a letter came from a graduate with a cheque for students' pocket money. It was used for this purpose.

Then followed rededication as we placed ourselves anew at the Lord's disposal.[9]

God had indeed answered their prayers for revival blessing, but in a manner they little expected. It was only a short while after this visitation that the Communists caused the seminary to be closed and the students scattered. How blessed that before they had to face the ordeal ahead, they had put things right with God and their fellowmen and had a clear sky above them.

Some years ago a great revival swept over Korea, the fruits of which revival remain to the present day. This revival had been prayed down. Four missionaries of different denominations had agreed to meet together to pray daily at noon. At the end of one month a brother proposed that "as nothing had happened," the prayer meetings should be discontinued. "Let us each pray at home as we find it convenient," said he. The others, however, protested that they ought rather to spend even more time in prayer each day. So they continued the daily prayer meetings for four months. Then suddenly the blessing began to be poured out.

In *Evangelical Christian* magazine, one of the missionaries declared: "It paid well to have spent several months in prayer; for when God gave the Holy Spirit, He accomplished more in half a day than all the missionaries together could have accomplished in half a year." In less than two months more than two thousand heathen were converted. In one church it was announced that a daily prayer meeting would be held every morning at 4:30. The very first day four hundred people arrived long before the stated hour, eager to pray. The number rapidly increased to six hundred. Heathen people came to see what was happening. They exclaimed in astonishment, "The living God is among you!"

When God plans to send revival blessing, He lays a burden for it on the hearts of those who make themselves available to Him. An aged saint came to his pastor one night and said, "We are about to have a revival." He was asked how he knew so. His answer was, "I went into the stable to take care of my cattle two hours ago, and there the Lord has kept me in prayer until just now. And I feel we are going to be revived." It proved to be the commencement of a revival. Are we similarly available?

PRAYER

O Lord, we pray for our country that God would bless it; and O that we might have a season of revival of pure and undefiled religion in the land. We perceive that Thou canst turn the hearts of the people, as the trees of the wood are moved in the wind. O that there might come a deep searching of heart, great thoughtfulness of the Scriptures, reverence of God and the principles of justice and peace; and may this land make another stride in onward progress, and out of it may there be gathered a people whom Thou hast chosen, who may show forth Thy praise.

CHARLES H. SPURGEON

QUESTIONS

1. Why do you think there appears to be such a close link between prayer and revival, although revival is a sovereign work of God?
2. Scripture appears to teach that we can see revival whenever we are willing to fulfill the conditions. Does history bear this out?

23

Review

Our school of prayer has concluded, but a life of prayer stretches out ahead. What we have learned in theory we must work out in daily praying, and this demands purpose of heart. God will not pray *instead* of us, but He will intercede *in* us and thus aid us in our weakness.

Let us now gather the lessons and principles of prayer that we have been learning.

1. Faith is an indispensable element, for "without faith it is impossible to please Him" (Heb 11:6; cf. Matt 17:20; James 1:6).
2. The petitioner must not be clinging to any sin. "If I regard wickedness in my heart, the Lord will not hear" (Psalm 66:18; cf. Isa 59:1-2).
3. To be effective, prayer must be offered in the name of Jesus. Implied in this is the understanding that the petitioner offers only requests that He could endorse. "Whatever you ask in My name, that will I do" (John 14:13; cf. 15:16; 16:23).
4. Our prayers must be in harmony with the will of God. "If we ask anything according to His will, He hears us" (1 John 5:14; cf. James 4:2-3).
5. Acceptable prayer is prayer in the Spirit—guided and directed by the Holy Spirit, who dispels spirit-

171

ual ignorance and imparts spiritual dynamics. "Praying in the Holy Spirit" (Jude 20; cf. Rom 8:26-27).

6. A forgiving spirit is essential to prevailing prayer. When a resentful or unforgiving spirit is harbored, the Spirit is grieved. Jesus frequently emphasized this principle. "And whenever you stand praying, forgive, if you have anything against anyone" (Mark 11:25; cf. Matt 6:12-15).

7. Importunity is another element God requires. "Ask, and it shall be given to you; seek, and you shall find; knock, and it shall be opened to you" (Luke 11:5-9; cf. 18:1-8).

8. To be effective, united prayer must flow from a Spirit-produced oneness of heart and mind. "If two of you agree [symphonize] on earth about anything that they may ask, it shall be done for them by My Father who is in heaven" (Matt 18:19).

9. There is an aggressive and militant side to prayer, which involves the intercessor in soul-travail and conflict if Satan's captives are to be delivered. "Our struggle is not against flesh and blood, but against . . . world forces of this darkness" (Eph 6:12; cf. Col 2:1).

10. Christ has delegated spiritual authority over Satan and his forces to His disciples, and we are encouraged to use this authority humbly in the spiritual warfare. "Behold, I have given you authority . . . over all the power of the enemy" (Luke 10:18-19). "They overcame him because of the blood of the Lamb and because of the word of their testimony, and they did not love their life even to death" (Rev 12:11).

Lord, teach us to pray.

Notes

CHAPTER 1

1. H. W. Frost, *Effective Praying* (Philadelphia: Sunday School Times, 1925), p. 21.
2. E. M. Bounds, *Prayer and Praying Men* (London: Hodder & Stoughton, 1921), p. 42.

CHAPTER 2

1. A. B. Bruce, cited by J. Gibb, "Thanksgiving," *The Outlook.*

CHAPTER 3

1. A. J. Courtney, "Prayer and the Prism," *Joyful News*, February 21, 1935, p. 1.

CHAPTER 5

1. E. F. and L. Harvey, *Kneeling We Triumph* (Blackburn, England: M.O.V.E. Press, 1971), p. 11.

CHAPTER 6

1. E. M. Bounds, *The Possibilities of Prayer* (New York: Revell, 1923), p. 24.
2. H. S. Curr, "Prayer and the Promises," in *Life of Faith* (London: Marshall, Morgan & Scott, 1941), p. 2
3. Report received by the O.M.F.

CHAPTER 7

1. D. M. M'Intyre, *In His Likeness* (London: Marshall, Morgan & Scott, n.d.), p. 28.

CHAPTER 8

1. S. Chadwick, *The Path of Prayer* (London: Hodder & Stoughton, 1936), p. 50.
2. Frost, *Effective Praying*, pp. 53-54.
3. Chadwick, *The Path of Prayer*, p. 52.

CHAPTER 9

1. S. M. Zwemer, *Into All the World* (Grand Rapids: Zondervan, 1943), p. 160.
2. H. W. Frost, "Praying in the Spirit," *Sunday School Times*, July 13, 1912.
3. Chadwick, *The Path of Prayer*, p. 56.
4. A. Murray, "Praying in the Spirit," *Alliance Weekly*, September 21, 1940, p. 597.
5. H. C. G. Moule, *The Epistle of Paul the Apostle to the Ephesians*, The Cambridge Bible for Schools and Colleges (Cambridge: Cambridge U., 1910), p. 159.
6. K. S. Wuest, *Ephesians and Colossians in the Greek New Testament* (Grand Rapids: Eerdmans, 1953), p. 145.
7. E. M. Bounds, *Purpose in Prayer* (New York: Revell, 1920), p. 123.

CHAPTER 10

1. W. E. Biederwolf, *How Can God Answer Prayer* (New York: Revell, 1910), p. 199.
2. Mrs. H. Taylor, *Behind the Ranges* (London: Lutterworth, 1944), pp. 108, 110, 112-13.
3. Ibid., p. 114.
4. G. Mueller, *The Diary of George Mueller*, ed. A. Rendle Short (Grand Rapids: Zondervan, 1972), p. 72.
5. J. O. Sanders, *Just the Same Today* (London: O.M.F., 1975), p. 20.
6. Ibid.

CHAPTER 11

1. Bounds, *Purpose in Prayer*, p. 54.
2. W. H. Aitken, *The Divine Ordinance of Prayer* (London: Wells Gardner, 1902), p. 118.
3. D. M. M'Intyre, *The Hidden Life of Prayer*, rev. ed. (Stirling, Scotland: Drummond's Tract Depot, n.d.), p. 120.

CHAPTER 12

1. H. A. Ironside, in *Serving and Waiting*, March 1930, p. 385.

CHAPTER 15

1. R. E. Speer, *Paul, the All-round Man* (New York: Revell, 1909), p. 91.
2. Ibid., p. 97.
3. S. F. Olford, *Heart-Cry for Revival* (Westwood, N. J.: Revell, 1962), pp. 83-84.
4. Speer, p. 92.

CHAPTER 16

1. Harvey and Harvey, *Kneeling We Triumph*, p. 66.
2. Chadwick, *The Path of Prayer*, pp. 20-21.
3. E. M. Bounds, *Power Through Prayer* (London: Marshall, Morgan & Scott, n.d.), p. 116.
4. Harvey and Harvey, p. 60.
5. Bounds, *Power Through Prayer*, p. 47.
6. A. J. Gordon, *The Holy Spirit and Missions* (New York: Revell, 1893), pp. 139-140.

CHAPTER 18

1. J. E. Orr, *Prayer, Its Deeper Dimensions* (London: Marshall, Morgan & Scott, 1963), p. 21.

CHAPTER 20

1. H. W. Frost, "What Is Scriptural Fasting," *Evangelical Christian*, January 1932, p. 24.
2. Harvey and Harvey, *Kneeling We Triumph*, p. 115.
3. O. Hallesby, *Prayer*, trans. C. J. Carlsen, 12th ed. (Minneapolis: Augsburg, 1935), p. 121.
4. Frost, "Scriptural Fasting," p. 24.
5. Ibid.
6. Mrs. H. Taylor, *Hudson Taylor* (London: China Inland Mission, 1918), p. 410.
7. Taylor, *Hudson Taylor*, p. 367.

Notes 175

CHAPTER 21

1. N. Deck, "Praying also for Us," *Alliance Weekly*, May 23, 1942, p. 322.
2. E. Purnell, "Women Missionaries and How to Pray for Them," *East Asia Millions*, February-March 1976, pp. 157-59.
3. *Challenge Newspaper* (Auckland, N.Z.), April 17, 1976.

CHAPTER 22

1. S. M. Zwemer, "The Psychology of Prayer," *Biblical Recorder*, August 1, 1922, p. 235.
2. Olford, *Heart-Cry for Revival*, pp. 28-29.
3. J. O. Sanders, *Expanding Horizons* (Auckland: Institute Press, 1971), p. 4.
4. Sanders, *Expanding Horizons*, p. 5.
5. W. Kemp, *Joseph W. Kemp* (London: Marshall, Morgan & Scott, n.d.), p. 30.
6. Sanders, *Expanding Horizons*, p. 6.
7. Kemp, p. 32.
8. Kemp, p. 30.
9. M. Cheng, *Lamp Aflame* (London: China Inland Mission, 1949).

Index of Persons Quoted